Customer Experience
Analytics

Dr. Arvind Sathi

MC PRESS

MC Press Online, LLC
Ketchum, ID 83340

Customer Experience Analytics: The Key to Real-Time, Adaptive Customer Relationships
By Dr. Arvind Sathi

First Edition
First Printing—October 2011

Every attempt has been made to provide correct information. However, the publisher and the author do not guarantee the accuracy of the book and do not assume responsibility for information included in or omitted from it.

The following terms are trademarks or registered trademarks of International Business Machines Corporation in the United States, other countries, or both: IBM, AIX, Cognos, Information Agenda, InfoSphere, Initiate, Optim, Redbooks, and SPSS. Netezza, Netezza Performance Server, NPS, and Twinfin are trademarks or registered trademarks of Netezza Corporation, an IBM Company.

Microsoft and PowerPoint are trademarks of Microsoft Corporation in the United States, other countries, or both.

Linux is a registered trademark of Linus Torvalds in the United States, other countries, or both. Other company, product, or service names may be trademarks or service marks of others.

MC Press offers excellent discounts on this book when ordered in quantity for bulk purchases or special sales, which may include custom covers and content particular to your business, training goals, marketing focus, and branding interest.

MC Press Online, LLC
    Corporate Offices
    P.O. Box 4886
    Ketchum, ID 83340-4886 USA
For information regarding sales and/or customer service, please contact:
    MC Press
    P.O. Box 4300
    Big Sandy, TX 75755-4300 USA
    Toll Free: (877) 226-5394
For information regarding permissions or special orders, please contact:
    mcbooks@mcpressonline.com

ISBN: 978-1-58347-344-3

Dedication

In fond memory of Prof. P. N. Thirunarayana, who introduced me to the fascinating world of Customer Experience Analytics nearly 34 years ago.

To Neena, Kinji, and Conal, who gave me the time, the encouragement, and support in writing this book.

About the Author

Dr. Arvind Sathi is the Global Communication Sector Lead Architect for the Information Agenda team at IBM®. Dr. Sathi received his Ph.D. in Business Administration from Carnegie Mellon University and worked under Nobel Prize winner Dr. Herbert A. Simon. Dr. Sathi is a seasoned professional with more than 20 years of leadership in Information Management architecture and delivery. His primary focus has been in the delivery and architecture oversight of IT projects to communications organizations. He has extensive experience with many domestic as well as international communications service providers, as well as with other services industries.

Prior to joining IBM, Dr. Sathi was the pioneer in developing knowledge-based solutions for CRM at Carnegie Group. At BearingPoint, he led the development of Enterprise Integration, MDM, and Operations Support Systems/Business Support Systems (OSS/BSS) solutions for the communications market and also developed horizontal solutions for communications, financial services, and public services. At IBM, Dr. Sathi has led several Information Management programs in MDM, data security, business intelligence, and related areas and has provided strategic architecture oversight to IBM's strategic accounts. He has also delivered a number of workshops and presentations at industry conferences on technical subjects including MDM and data architecture, and he holds patents in data masking.

Acknowledgements

First and foremost, I would like to acknowledge the hard work from the Information Agenda community in creating a world-class reference material. I have heavily referenced the material here, including the Business Maturity Model, the Solution Architecture framework, and a number of case studies. I would like to acknowledge Bob Keseley, Wayne Jensen, and Mick Fullwood for conceiving the ideas and organizing the reference material. I would like to acknowledge Tim Davis for his encouragement and for providing financial services examples. The technical ideas were created with help from Paul Christensen, Beth Brownhill, Elizabeth Dial, Noman Mohammed, Rich Harken, Tommy Eunice, Daryl BC Peh, and Sam Iyer. Mehul Shah, Emeline Tjan, Steve Trigg, Don Bahash, and Jessica White have provided valuable business value analysis components in this book. I would like to thank the Communication Sector Industry Consulting team, Ken Kralick, Dirk Michelsen, Tushar Mehta, Richard Lanahan, Rick Flamand, Linda Moss, and David Buck for providing the opportunities, customers, and contributions to the CEA solutions. I am grateful to Anant Jhingran, Hamid Pirahesh, and Seeta Hariharan for their encouragement as I developed the material for this book and presented the CEA story.

Next, I would like to acknowledge the excellent work from the IBM Business Analytics and Optimization consulting team. In particular, Ravesh Lala, Aparna Betigeri, and Neena Sathi provided the ideas behind the Master Data Management (MDM) chapter through their consulting. I would also like to thank Mark Holste for collaborations and brainstorms on these solutions. John

Held provided me with very valuable insight into predictive modeling, and the section on predictive modeling includes a number of his ideas and figures.

The IBM Software Group product teams provided the much-needed case studies and product examples. I would like to thank Roger Rea for his help on the InfoSphere® Streams product, Maria Diecidue for her support towards MDM and Initiate®, Andrew Colby for help on the Netezza® Analytics Engine, Claudio Zancani for Optim™ Privacy, and Mike Zucker for SPSS®.

I would like to thank Rajit Johri for a very insightful discussion regarding my Honda Insight and for providing me with automobile research information from his Ph.D. thesis.

I would like to acknowledge Anthony Behan for a number of thought-provoking ideas that went into my definition of Customer Experience Analytics.

I worked closely with the practitioners as I studied CEA business opportunities. This includes Azhar Mirza, Benafsha Irani, Bob Speer, Brian Clements, Carmen Allen, Dick LaRue, Imran Jan, Kedrick Brown, Gautam Shah, George Krieg, Jessica Ma, Jim Hicks, John Stacey, Josh Morton, Joshua Koran, Judith List, Krishnan Narayan, Lindsey Pardun, Mahesh Dalvi, Maria Pardee, Melodi Gates, Nick Carnovale, Nick Richmond, Sandeep Kulkarni, Steve Ward, Sumit Chowdhury, Sumit Singh, Teresa Jacobs, Tom Deffet, and Vinny Clements. I am grateful for the insightful discussions and implementations in understanding business opportunities as well as architectures for CEA. I would like to thank Girish Varma, Harsch Bhatnagar, and Sami Syed for their guidance and review of the book.

I would like to thank Sunil Soares for inspiring me to write the book. Gaurav Deshpande did a fair amount of work behind the scenes to help me get the book organized and funded. Susan Visser provided valuable help in organizing the publication process. Katie Tipton provided valuable publication and editorial guidance.

Last, but not least, I would like to thank my wife Neena Sathi, my daughter Kinji Sathi, and my son Conal Sathi for their inspiration, support, and editorial help.

Contents

Foreword

Telecommunications service providers are facing unprecedented data growth, which presents both a challenge and an opportunity. Data growth brings significant increases in storage, licenses, and IT staff costs, as well as triage in business units using the data. The ability to convert data into a strategic asset while reducing data management costs is what differentiates leaders from laggards. While data analytics can be used for a number of business functions, the best place to use it is to improve our interaction with the customer.

Most businesses have more meaningful data about their customers than they realize. Aggregation and analysis of this data can lead to enormous insights about customers, their needs, and how they would like the business to interact with them. Using this asset effectively can enable a business to provide a complete customer experience that sets it apart from other providers who deliver just a product or service.

My IT organization manages more than three petabytes of data growing over 40 percent a year. We have been working hard at converting this data into useful information to improve our customers' experience. Over the past four years, we have invested in more than 50 projects that use customer/ product data to improve operational capabilities across the entire customer and product life cycle. These projects have led us to a deeper understanding of our customers. This has enabled us to customize our interactions with them to deliver a better experience while improving our operational cost.

Our call centers handle more than 100,000 customer conversations per day. We collate information about a customer's products, trouble calls, payment history, and demographics, including whether they are a family with many devices, an early technology adopter, or a long-time landline customer, into a 360-degree view for our service representatives. This allows them to focus their attention on the customer and not on collating this information while on the call. The representatives can now personalize customer interaction and recommend additional products and services that would meet the customer's need. This data is also used to route the call to appropriate representatives through our IVR system, reducing wait time or transferring the customer from one representative to another. The resulting improvement in customer experience is evidenced by sales numbers that exceeded our business case estimates. We have also used this deeper understanding of our customer to improve marketing campaigns, product and service design, invoice design, fraud detection, et cetera—leading to lower operational cost and improved customer experience.

I first met Arvind while I was leading the Telecom Center of Excellence at IBM several years ago. Arvind showed a lot of dedication and insight into assembly and use of information. As we started to build the strategic blue print at Qwest, we sought his help in bringing the best practices and industry experience in implementing analytics applications. Arvind has worked closely with our architects and development teams on a number of these initiatives. He also works with other service providers and has been able to assemble many case studies and best practices. His book is the best representation of this combined knowledge of Customer Experience Analytics problems and solutions.

My personal interest has always been to represent information technology capabilities in business terms. This book does an excellent job of presenting Customer Experience Analytics in business terms, using interesting case studies and relevant examples. There are always two audiences for such books: business executives who have business needs and seek technologies for solutions, and technologists who seek to build the right solution to address a business need. This book does a great job of addressing both audiences and provides rich information to both sides. I strongly recommend this as reading material for any one buried under customer and product data and wanting to make a change in the way information can be used to transform customer experience.

Dr. Girish Varma
Executive Vice President—
Information Technology Services,
CenturyLink

Introduction

Analytics is one of the hottest topics of interest among organizations worldwide not only to information technology (IT) but also sales and marketing professionals. Applying analytics to customer experience provides the highest business value to an organization and is often the most sought-after IT application.

IBM has declared analytics to be one of the four most important areas of growth toward its 2015 plan. IBM has made significant investments in both research and development (R&D) as well as in external acquisition to infuse both organic and inorganic growth in this area. In the latest research with chief marketing officers (CMOs), 67 percent of 1,000 survey recipients reported an intention to increase their investment in customer analytics. This is the highest among all areas of investment reported in the study.[1]

The market for customer experience is morphing. In the 1990s, a number of companies initiated packaging and selling of Customer Relationship Management (CRM) solutions that covered marketing, sales, and customer service aspects. In the late 1990s and early 2000s, Master Data Management (MDM) and related topics became popular. *Customer Experience Analytics* (CEA) is a continuation of this journey as it comprehensively covers sales, product usage, and billing experience and correlates them for a more thorough understanding from the customer view. Furthermore, CEA uses this initial analysis to impact policies, procedures, and customer communication.

What Is Good Customer Experience?

Let us start the discussion with an understanding of good customer experience. In our daily lives, we come across hundreds of companies. With all the automation and multi-touch points, we often encounter good or bad interactive voice responses (IVRs), web sites, and call centers as we deal with our services providers, whether they are banks, airlines, telecommunications companies, investment brokers, or health care providers. We spend hours pouring out our experiences into social networking sites for others to know whether we liked a restaurant, a holiday resort, or a store. It does not take a long time for us to observe, judge, and differentiate good or bad customer experience. We often return to the organizations that provide good customer experience, and we declare it publicly by selecting the "like" option on Facebook.

How do we characterize good customer experience, and how can it be sensed by the serving organization? What makes us like or dislike an organization so much that we explore public ways of expressing it?

First Impressions

Fred Wiersema has posed six important questions:[2]

1. Can your customers find you?
2. Is your first impression memorable?
3. Do you get in the way when people are buying?
4. Are you sending unintended messages?
5. Are your products intuitive?
6. Do you show your customers a united front?

As we move from brick-and-mortars to e-commerce, these first impressions are still important in consumer purchase criteria. A lot depends on how we judge a product or service through our first impressions. This point is true not only for impulsive purchases but also for well-thought-out, well-researched, big-ticket items. We look for simplicity and respect in our first interactions. We look for memorable experiences. We sometimes eliminate products based on simple and trivial criteria.

The questions listed above are easy starters to understand and differentiate a good customer experience from a bad one. So how do we analyze and differentiate between a "memorable" experience and a "bad" experience? Fortunately, customer touch points provide us with a lot of associated data: How many customers abandon purchases after reaching shopping carts? How many times do we ask customers to type the same information? How much do we trust our customers? Do customers stop shopping when we start asking for a credit-card number during a free trial? In our highly instrumented customer experiences, some of this associated data can be collected, collated, and analyzed. It provides us with insights about how the customer is perceiving the product and the customer contact.

Service on Customer Terms

In today's automated world, customers like to receive service on their terms. If I value *self-service*, I would be delighted to find my bank account fully accessible to me after dinner for any transaction. However, if the only way I deal with a bank is to visit the friendly bank branch in my neighborhood, the late-night web site access provides me with no extra value. If I have a complex customer relationship with my broker with many accounts for many members of my household, integrating all the accounts under a single login would be great. However, if I have a single account, I do not need account consolidation.

Over the years, many hotels tried copying the Ritz Carlton Hotels' legendary capability to remember past customer experience with the hotel chain, including little details across visits, so that service would be personalized and enriched for customers making frequent visits. Does every customer like that level of personalization? For my short business trips, I am interested only in a speedy check-in, and I often ignore the poor clerk peering through his screen and saying "It is nice to see you back" or remembering a preference I expressed once in a blue moon and have no reason to replicate.

If I reach the hospital in an emergency, my expectation for a warm welcome is a fast check-in process and rapid delivery of medical expertise. Folks at a call center organization in India once told me they send birthday greetings to all their customers. They were confused when many of their customers gave them the feedback that they would rather receive fast service than a birthday greeting card.

How do we discover these customer expectations and preferences? How do we measure and improve customer experience by aligning our products and services to what customers expect?

Customer Differentiation

We have customers, and then we have premium and VIP customers. We often break rules for our most important customers or, better still, have different rules for different levels of customers, thereby rewarding those who provide us with the heaviest revenue. A leading telecommunications organization found that 8 percent of its customers contributed 45 percent to its revenue. Any churn among these 8 percent customers represented a major revenue impact. At the same time, cultivating and harnessing such premium customers gives us the best way to protect our revenue base.

Premium customers are not always that easy to identify. Members of a household may make purchases using their individual accounts; however, money and decision-making might be centralized or collaborative. Changes in marital status or kids off to college may continue to follow old accounts despite new hierarchies. As employees of corporations make personal purchases using discounts offered through corporations, and then leave one job to join another, customer accounts go with the employee—with or without the discounting—depending on how we track the corporate accounts. One of my publishing customers told me that a large number of the company's corporate customers use public emails for customer communications. It was not clear to them which customers were using proper corporate subscriptions. As we move to medium and large enterprises as customers, finding premium customers is even more challenging amid departmental or corporate contracts, mergers and acquisitions, and other corporate events. How do we stitch the customer experience and payment information together to identify and manage our premium customers?

In addition to the customers, the supplier customer records may be equally broken down. How do we find these customers, if the revenue is counted in different ways in different business units or if the customer definition changes from one business unit to the next? Let us say that we have identified the premium customers. Do we now have a way to provide differentiated services to them? How do we design policies that differentiate these customers? How do we apply these policies consistently across the touch points, so that the premium customers feel the difference? How do we measure whether the differences lead to an impact in customer loyalty level?

Management of Opinions and Sentiments

A century ago, all calls were routed by operators. Each operator knew the people who called by name and knew their personal details. Bank employees knew their customers by name and face. I remember walking to an airline gate just two decades ago, and the airline staff bent their rules to let me board an airplane in the middle of Christmas rush because I was their most frequent traveler that year. As organizations have consolidated and automated their customer-facing functions, this personal touch has disappeared. However, the positive and negative sentiments are still present in the buyer–seller interactions.

Would a self-service system provide me with a personal touch? How do we express empathy via a web site? How do we identify an angry customer or a destructive buzz in the marketplace? How do we analyze and sense customer sentiment and use the information to drive better customer service? While a service provider may offer a faceless web site, the customers can gripe about it on Facebook or Yelp.

I got hooked to an Indian TV show and found it had a fan club on Facebook. In this case, the fan club members were in their teens and early 20s, and they were drawn to the show because it depicted the story of office romance and humor. Facebook provided a perfect channel for them to discuss the show and offer opinions back to the performers. However, someone not very familiar with the power of Facebook decided to convert the show into a family drama. It was fascinating to watch the sentiment transform overnight with negative comments, petitions to boycott the show, and appeals to the writers to change the show. As we can easily expect, the show was soon canceled because it could not manage the negative sentiment and demands to change the story and the focus of the show.

More recently, we have seen Facebook and other social networking sites, such as YouTube and Twitter, provide important media outlets for political change in the Middle East. We should recognize customer sentiment in social networks during product launches and use it to fix product problems.

Analytics to Drive Customer Experience

The business capabilities offered through analytics are changing rapidly. Customers are increasingly connected with their suppliers using a variety of electronic touch points—web browsers, interactive voice response, wireless devices, and kiosks are a few examples. Customer experience can be altered through these electronic touch points in real-time. Also, customers have access to a variety of methods to publicly express their satisfaction or disappointment, in real-time worldwide. The associated data is accumulated by the supplier organizations in petabytes. This data must be sorted, correlated, analyzed, and acted upon rapidly and intelligently to make a positive, long-lasting impact on the customer. Last but not least, it is no longer sufficient to report customer problems to an analyst who routes to business owners on a monthly basis. The actions must be inserted in appropriate customer-facing service, sales, billing, or operational functions to alter customer experience—often in near real-time. While the Internet has provided enormous power to consumers, the business markets have also gained an enormous amount of sophistication in multi-supplier management, electronic gateways, and customer and product data across the supply food chain.

Corporations are struggling with legacy systems that do not meet this fast-paced, action-oriented requirement from their business and consumer markets. We need a program with a solid basis in business values that appeals to the senior management, a road map that charts the way, and a solution architecture that utilizes the fast, intelligent, and action-packed CEA capabilities.

Sources of Study Material

Over the past 30 years, I have been in the business of developing customer experience. My major work is in explaining technical ideas to nontechnical audiences to gain their commitment and support for large, mission-critical CEA implementations. I also bring personal experience in designing and building CEA solutions across the globe in a number of industries. Using a series of case studies from a variety of industries, this book will demonstrate transformation to a world-class customer experience.

Under Bob Keseley's leadership, IBM created an Information Agenda® program that offers business and technical advice to customers regarding use of IT for analytics. In the two years that the Information Agenda team has been in business, they have seen CEA grow as the most important area of analytics. They have also seen a strong demand for CEA ideas and best practices. The Information Agenda team has conducted over 500 workshops and has accumulated an enormous understanding of the market for CEA. There is a global interest in these solutions, as each quarter, they share workshop reports created in German, Japanese, Mandarin, Spanish, French, and other languages. There is also a growing interest and action in the growth markets. The case studies and the methodologies reported in this book heavily draw upon the Information Agenda intellectual assets, products, references, and case studies.

While there is an enormous demand for CEA, most organizations are constrained in their ability to develop systems that span many divisions and geographies. Many legal and political challenges exist, with customer data privacy being one of the most important areas of concern. These organizations also require collaboration across entities known to work as silos before. We are also seeing coalitions across companies to create new information markets, where each company delivers a small portion of the overall information pie to be integrated and consumed by the end users. The case studies and best practices provided here have identified business capabilities enabled by CEA, if we can break the barriers and start to assemble an integrated understanding of the customer. These business capabilities have enabled organizations to build significant competitiveness and in many cases bring disruptive changes in the marketplace.

CEA is a continuum. What may be the target state for one organization is a starting point for another. At times, we do not have business justification for going beyond a certain level of sophistication. I have introduced maturity levels to acknowledge this continuum.

Book Organization and Intended Audience

The book includes three major segments. The first segment introduces the concept of Customer Experience Analytics using a series of customer experience scenarios. It discusses three enablers for CEA: automation in customer-facing processes and products, customer use of CEA data for decision-making, and emerging markets for customer data that are fueling a monetization of customer experience information. It also addresses regulatory concerns and changes coming rapidly to govern the movement of customer data. The second segment covers the CEA solution—including Master Data Management, Data Movement, Stream Computing, Analytics Engines, Predictive Modeling, and Privacy Management. This section also includes key technical contributions each area is making to the overall CEA solution. The third section provides a mechanism to establish the program, identify value, and measure progress.

This book is intended for a semi-technical audience. It uses a series of scenarios, case studies, and allegories to illustrate the CEA business opportunity, solution, and program. The technical terms are defined for easy reference. I have chosen consumer scenarios and pulled everyday examples from my own experiences. I have provided selected "deep dives" into technical details to help readers understand the technologies in the context of the solution. While business-to-business markets provide rich scenarios, I hope to cover them in a separate book or white paper.

This book is intended for two distinct audiences, each of which may read the book for different reasons. The technical community understands its products and how they are used. The business community has interesting problems and is in search of technologies. Very often, the technical community has good understanding of point products but not the end-to-end architecture for a solution. Similarly, the business community has a good understanding of immediate business requirements but not a full awareness of how technology can be used to bring disruptive changes in the marketplace. Occasionally, we see entrepreneurial organizations coming up with an innovative use of the technology bridging to a major business need, leading to a complete overhaul of the marketplace. CEA is at the cusp of such an upheaval, and this book addresses both audiences in providing them each other's views.

The first target audience for this book is senior to mid management level in sales operations, marketing, strategy, or IT. These organizations typically participate in the Customer Experience Analytics solutions. In particular, financial services, public services, health care, telecom, energy and utilities, and electronics companies will find the most use from this book, as these groups have strong market pulls and strategic gains from implementing CEA. They will find tangible ideas to implement within their organization and gain insights about how to sell the CEA program in their organization. Using case studies and trends in the first half, the book illustrates business problems faced by this group and, in relatively simple terms, shows essential solution components for defining their solutions.

The second target audience is the IT service and software provider community. This group includes IT consultants who are engaged in developing CEA solutions, software organizations developing products, and cloud vendors building hosted solutions for CEA. The second half of the book shows this community how their technologies are combined to form an end-to-end solution. This group will also find the first half of the book useful in exploring the business scenarios addressed by these solutions. They will get an understanding of the end-to-end business opportunity, solution architecture, and where their component fits into the end-to-end solution.

PART ONE:

The CEA Opportunity

CHAPTER

1

The Industry View

In this chapter, we introduce customer experience and Customer Experience Analytics (CEA) using a set of industry examples. Each industry has a different name for its customers—subscribers, citizens, patients, drivers, viewers, and so on. However, the examples will illustrate similar characteristics. In each case, customer data is collected and harnessed to create insights about the customers, using a set of predictive models. The enriched information is used to drive improvements in products or customer-facing processes. In each industry example, I have chosen examples that are personal and commonplace, so we can relate easily to them and realize the level of disruptive change they can bring to suppliers around us.

Customer Experience Analytics Through Examples

Davenport and Harris have defined *analytics* to mean "the extensive use of data, statistical and quantitative analysis, explanatory and predictive models, and fact-based management to derive decisions and actions."[3] Let us use a set of industry examples to show how analytics as defined by Davenport and Harris is being applied to a number of consumer-facing industries. We encounter good as well as bad customer experience from a variety of suppliers. While each of us may have different measures for evaluating customer experience, we can easily spot good encounters based on the attention, personalization, trust, or emotional attachment a supplier provides to us. Some suppliers are far better at analyzing our experience and using that understanding to improve their product, customer service, price, location, et cetera. The experience is pervasive across a cross-section of industries (see Figure 1.1).

Imagine If Decision Makers Could...

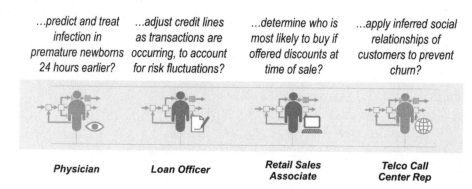

| ...predict and treat infection in premature newborns 24 hours earlier? | ...adjust credit lines as transactions are occurring, to account for risk fluctuations? | ...determine who is most likely to buy if offered discounts at time of sale? | ...apply inferred social relationships of customers to prevent churn? |

| **Physician** | **Loan Officer** | **Retail Sales Associate** | **Telco Call Center Rep** |

...optimize every transaction, process, and decision at the point of impact, based on the current situation, without requiring that every customer-facing person be the analytical expert

Figure 1.1: CEA across many industries

Let me take a couple of industries to narrate customer experiences and how analytics is used to organize, collate, mine, and improve customer experience. Using a set of case studies, I will show how customer data is organized, analyzed, and incorporated into business decisions.

Communication Service Providers

Let me start with our experience as communications customers. We all have often experienced issues related to call and Internet data quality. In June 2010 at Apple's Worldwide Developers Conference (WWDC), CEO Steve Jobs decided to demonstrate video conferencing capabilities on the iPhone. As he was connecting his iPhone to demonstrate the video calling features, the connection failed. Because this was Steve Jobs demonstrating a new cool feature, you can be sure that the hundreds of reporters and analysts sitting in the room were each connected to the facility's Wi-Fi and trying to upload the news and related information to their respective sites. Unfortunately, this crowding of devices took a toll on the device Steve Jobs was using. As he tried repeatedly to connect his iPhone, the connection kept failing. It is important to note that in this case the problem causing the dropped calls was right in the room, not with a communications service provider, a device, or an application running on a device. The video shows the problem getting fixed as Steve Jobs repeatedly tells the audience to shut down their devices.

The IT support organization deserves a big accolade for identifying the problem with the failed connections in near real-time. Steve Jobs was persistent in fixing the problem. After trying to connect a couple more times, he asked the audience to disconnect their devices so he could proceed with the demo. You can watch a video clip of his attempts to fix the problem on YouTube at *http://www.youtube.com/watch?v=RGVsGSimLJg.*

Although this particular example was not caused by the service provider, our gut reaction would be to be to blame the service provider. I asked some of the communications service providers how they keep track of their premium and VIP customers, how they excel in their service to their most important customers, and how they manage their customer perception for premium customers. Traditionally, Service Level Agreements (SLAs) were managed through service contracts. Most wireless providers traditionally offered loyalty points or service discounts if they faced service problems. For mass markets, that may be a good start. However, as the Steve Jobs video demonstrates, this case involved a very important wireless device, whose failure would be openly discussed by analysts and posted on YouTube.

How do we know the calls were dropped? The information is available to a service provider. Are they analyzing this information to trigger corrective actions before the service reaches a level of intolerance? As we see in the video, Steve Jobs made repeated attempts during the demonstration. Could we count five dropped calls and trigger a response once we reach that threshold, especially when dealing with premium customers? How do we know if five dropped calls is a normal threshold for customer churn? How do we identify the service performance to the phone owner? How do we know that the service interruption is impacting a premium customer? The cause of a dropped call could be anything, whether it is the service provider network, the roaming network, or the device.

Clearly, service providers cannot monitor every subscriber and provide personalized attention. Is it possible for us to differentiate service for the best customers? How do we prioritize network operations to deal with premium customers first? The information about the service interruption is being generated in real-time. Can we collect this information, correlate with premium customers, analyze to establish root cause, and work with the subscriber to fix the problem? Can we work on this in near real-time so the subscriber may start receiving better performance right away? Can we involve the sales teams, the customer service organization, the touch points, and the device, so all of them are aware of the problem and are helping the subscriber in solving the problem?

I often work from my home office if I am not traveling to client sites, and I often need to download large documents. I decided on a 10 Mbps DSL line to reduce the download time on these large files. Unfortunately, much to my dismay, downloads remained painfully slow. I was on the verge of calling my cable company to experiment with cable modems. Unexpectedly, I received a call from my telecommunications service provider. The caller introduced himself as a network operations person and told me he was concerned that I was getting only 10 percent performance on my DSL line. He asked me if I had any analog devices connected to the phone line without a DSL filter. After surveying the house, I found that my home security alarm system was connected to the phone line directly, without the DSL filter. He told me that I needed to contact my home security provider for a special filter.

After a little bit of discussion, I decided to go for a second line instead, so that I could dedicate a line to my home office. I was promptly transferred to the customer service representative (CSR). In my discussion with the CSR, I discovered that I was using a metered long-distance product that offered me monthly calls up to a certain number of minutes. At the same time, I was hitting the upper limit each month due to my business calls from the home phone. By moving to an unlimited plan, I reduced the communications service provider's task of reporting a log of my long-distance calls, and I saved myself $10 per month. Eventually, I decided to apply the $10 toward getting a 20 Mbps DSL service.

What happened here? I had a sub-optimal telephone configuration for my needs, and I was a perfect candidate to churn. The call from network operations not only saved me as a customer but also increased the revenue through a second line and made the service far closer to my requirements. The service I received was very personalized. The call was totally unsolicited but based on specific performance data from my line. My discussion with the CSR was equally interesting. Instead of just selling a second line to me, he used information about my usage to compare products for me and offer me one that saved me money and was more useful.

As competition and cost pressures have intensified, corporations worldwide are on a mission to improve customer service and reduce operational costs using technology. Unfortunately, for a number of years, the pendulum kept shifting toward cost reduction. Process consultants clocked every second of call center time and every transaction in customer service, looking for ways to reduce sales costs. The end result was multiple hierarchies of IVR trees, impersonal call centers, and rigorous implementation of organizational policies—ending in poor customer experience.

My experience above is very contrary to this cost-cutting trend. The customer-facing personnel used precious time to patiently work with me on my requirements, finding problems with my installation and the billing options currently on my plan. They offered me recommendations that improved my service and their future prospects for keeping me as a long-time customer. In doing so, they relied heavily on information about me known to them—products purchased and their subsequent usage. Also, they were supported by their data warehouse and analytics applications, which pinpointed to them that they were at risk of losing me, a premium customer, due to the trickle feed I was getting on my bandwidth. They were able to focus on customers with high revenue and the highest risk of defection.

Financial Institutions

Let me now move to the financial services industry. For my house, I had a home mortgage as well as a home equity line. While both loans came from the same mortgage provider, they were sold to me separately, and I ended up setting up online access to both accounts. I had two different user names and passwords, and each time I accessed my account to make changes, such as cell phone contact information, I had to repeat the changes in both accounts. One fine morning, I logged into my home mortgage account and found that the home equity account was now showing up along with the home mortgage account in a single login.

My bank had used a Master Data Management (MDM) program to consolidate mortgage accounts. My account was a perfect candidate to be discovered in the "harmonization process." Both accounts had the same name, social security number, phone number, and address. The only task the bank had was to seek my authorization, and now I was relieved from double typing changes to both accounts.

At the height of the real estate bubble, we all excitedly purchased houses, looking for the lowest mortgage rates. Banks competed bravely, converting mortgages into commodities to be traded as securities. What happened to the customer experience? Mortgage shopping for the lowest interest rate resulted in multiple accounts.

Mortgage companies have limited visibility to our overall portfolio. Between my house and rental property, I have four mortgage loans with three different mortgage providers. In addition, I have two banks helping me with my cash accounts. Any time a change occurs in my personal information, I have to enter it in five places. I am the ultimate information integrator. Each of these five providers has a very small window of visibility to my portfolio and, hence, no ability to offer any consolidations. At the same time, an enormous opportunity exists for any one of them to increase their share of the wallet, if they could show me an integrated front. This happened to my bank; they discovered I had two loans with them, and I found it easier to deal with them, which should positively impact my future mortgage company selection in their favor.

As I studied the problem, I discovered yet another reason for my bank to consolidate my accounts. Banks are very concerned about the overall risk associated with a customer. As we take mortgages, use their investment arms for margin calls, and take auto and home equity loans, we are increasingly making the bank vulnerable to household risk of failure. If the housing market slides and leads to a foreclosure on the house as well as a bankruptcy, all the accounts related to the individual are impacted. The cleanup begins with the accounts held with the same bank. If using a harmonization process, the bank can discover all the accounts the individual has with the bank, and the risk can then be computed at the household level.

By analyzing social media data, we can discover household relationships, as well as business relationships across individuals. This data can be used for far more accurate computation of overall risk. This information can also be used to identify fraudulent behaviors or money laundering, and for other risk-related identity applications.

Banks can combine their data with outside data to gain an accurate understanding of the customer. Credit-card operations for a bank are good candidates for this total real-time view of the customer. Credit-card companies have invested significantly in fraud-detection systems. These systems operate in near real-time and evaluate each transaction made by a customer using the customer's past historical purchase record—time of purchase, location, type of purchase, and transaction value, to name a few. Any deviations from the past are examined closely and accepted or rejected based on rules accumulated over years of fraud detection. The solution has a real-time analytics component, which provides the capability to evaluate a transaction while the transaction is being processed. It also has a predictive modeling component that creates fraud-detection rules based on analysis of historical data. Credit-card operators constantly monitor the effectiveness of these rules and modify them based on their success in detecting fraud while maintaining a good customer experience in the use of credit cards. If the fraud detection resulted in questioning of every transaction, it would drive up the execution costs and imperil customer experience. If fraud detection resulted in the passage of fraudulent transactions, it would drive losses to the credit-card operators and customers. The optimization involves a fast real-time analytics engine and an ability to use predictive modeling to further modify this engine.

My work requires me to travel frequently, almost once a week. While traveling, I use my corporate card all the time and use my personal credit card sparingly—using it only when I need to make any personal purchases. This behavior poses a problem to the real-time analytics and monitoring of my personal card because the usage is sporadic and geographically diverse in a random manner. Invariably, the credit card is denied at the time of purchase, requiring me to phone the call center for security verification. These calls are expensive. I remember talking to a support line three times from India, with each call taking ten minutes or longer. The overall cost of the call, including telephone charges, the call center agent's time, and my time, adds up.

While I am thankful to the credit-card company for taking my card security seriously, I was curious whether there was an easier way for them to deal with me. I asked the credit-card call center agent how I could make the card company's monitoring easier, and the response was to call them before each trip. This solution might reduce the number of times my credit card is denied; however, it would significantly increase the call-center costs. And I would have to call each time before traveling, which could be a lot more than the number of times I use my personal credit card, or the times credit is denied.

The premise for credit-card fraud is that someone could steal my credit card and use it. A typical fraud rule looks for an unusual purchase initiated in an international location. Unfortunately, for frequent travelers like me, regular credit-card use can easily mimic these fraudulent transactions. As I travel to Mexico frequently but use my personal credit card rarely, each of those purchases is very likely to be tagged as unusual activity. However, I carry a credit card and a smart phone all the time when I travel. Although my credit-card company may not know of my travel to distant geographies, my smart phone has full awareness of my location. Also, the chances of my losing both my credit card and my phone are significantly less. If only I could authorize my credit-card company to check my phone location each time there is a concern about the credit-card usage, and even place an app on my phone to ask me to authorize the charges using a secure login or password to eliminate possibility of my phone being stolen at the same time.

Financial institutions are rapidly discovering their partnership with the phone companies. Today, Chase offers mobile check deposit using the Apple iPhone.[4] Using the camera in an iPhone, I can take a picture of both sides of the check and then use the Chase Mobile app on my iPhone to log into my account with a special authorization ID supplied by Chase. Now that my phone and bank are aware of each other, they can use this information for a variety of applications to improve my customer experience.

Public Services

The risk and credit-card fraud analytics covered above for the financial services has another set of buyers: federal, state, and local government, who analyze money laundering, tax fraud, and related criminal activities. The losses due to fraud are enormous. These losses can stem from tax evasion, misappropriation of funds, or fraudulent benefit applications. CEA can provide public services with the tools to enable fraud analytics using predictive models and the enormous social media and third-party data available to them

Over the past couple of years, we have seen a rapid growth in misuse of technology for organizing "flash mobs." In a typical flash mob, the suspects often connect via cell phones or social media sites and converge on a spot to engage in stealing goods from stores or assaulting bystanders. *USA Today* reported on one such incident in August: "Philadelphia leaders imposed an early curfew on parts of the city this month after roving bands of teens beat and robbed bystanders during violent attacks across the city. Surveillance cameras caught several dozen youths swarming into convenience stores in Germantown, Maryland, and Washington, D.C., and stealing armfuls of snacks and drinks as the store clerk looked on helplessly."[5]

This is a use of technology that originated from the unrest in the Middle East. While Middle East youths used the Internet effectively to fight their dictators, its spread for criminal activities must be controlled by law enforcement agencies. This enforcement requires a use of technology. It would require use of CEA to sense group activities in public forums and cell phones and identify any activities associated with criminal intent. Unfortunately, collecting and analyzing such data may be considered a violation of citizens' privacy rights.

Health Care

All of us have a vested interest in knowing that the healthcare systems are capable of taking care of their patients. CEA plays a big role in aligning support information to improve patient care (i.e., customer experience). This task starts with improving availability of patient data. Countries the world over are embracing e-health initiatives that can bring more efficiency to health systems. In the United States, the American Recovery and Reinvestment Act (ARRA) is providing seed money and other initiatives to expand adoption of electronic medical records. There are many examples of organizations and governments on the forefront of healthcare transformation. One exceptional organization is the University of Pittsburgh Medical Center (UPMC).

UPMC has been at the forefront of healthcare IT and redefining models of healthcare delivery. A model for Health Information Exchange (HIE), UPMC serves 29 western Pennsylvania counties, supported by more than 45,000 employees, 20 hospitals, and 400 physician offices/outpatient centers. In a typical year, UPMC has more than 167,000 inpatient admissions, 3 million outpatient visits, and 400,000 emergency visits. UPMC serves the health needs of more than 4 million people each year. The IT environment is similarly large and complex, with over 1,100 IT professionals supporting more than 2,000 applications. A solid foundation for health information exchange begins with the ability to safely share the wealth of patient data across the UPMC environment. For this, UPMC needed a proven and trusted Enterprise Master Patient Index (EMPI).

Nine source systems of person/patient data, seven source systems of provider data, and one source of organization information are part of the new EMPI that serves as the foundation for patient and provider identification across clinical and administrative systems throughout the UPMC network. UPMC now has the ability to manage not only person data but also data for providers and organizations within a single application. The solution comprises three different entities: people (patients), providers, and organizations. It harmonizes more than 8 million records across 17 distinct resources and conducts over 1.8 million weekly transactions.

UPMC is helping to revolutionize healthcare information exchange and interoperability. In June 2011, UPMC announced that it had begun sharing data with the Pennsylvania Immunization Registry to improve patient health. UPMC has created one of the first systems in the state to not only provide real-time, electronic reporting to Pennsylvania's immunizations registry but also to allow UPMC's clinicians to view the state's vaccine data for each patient.

UPMC's technology team, working with IBM and its systems integration partner Summa, created a computer interface that allows clinicians to match information from Pennsylvania Statewide Immunization Information System (PA-SIIS) to any individual patient and to include that data when viewing a patient's electronic health record at UPMC. The system links patient identity data from numerous sources. Inpatient, outpatient, and state data are provided to caregivers in a single application. Thus, physicians and nurses are able to see immunizations that might have been given outside UPMC's own network of doctors and hospitals, including those provided by pharmacy-based clinics or employee health departments.

Since implementing the new health interoperability and intelligence solution, the University of Pittsburgh Medical Center has seen a significant improvement in patient care, treatment outcomes, and administrative efficiencies. Physicians and nurses now spend much less time searching for information, which not only streamlines activities but also speeds patient care. For instance, the time required to collect preoperative information has been reduced by 80 percent, leading to a 50 percent increase in patient readiness for surgery while also reducing surgical wait times.

"The Pennsylvania immunization registry is the single source of truth for vaccination information, and a critical part of preventing the spread of diseases and premature deaths," says Lisa Khorey, vice president of enterprise systems and data management at UPMC. "The integration we created from our health system to the state supports our entire patient population with no burden on the clinician to manually enter data. This nearly two-year effort by UPMC's technology team, in collaboration with dedicated state employees, will help UPMC to meet complex federal requirements to show 'meaningful use' of electronic health records using data exchange," notes Ms. Khorey. "More importantly, participating in the state registry supports public health while providing coordinated care for our patients."

Another benefit is improved patient care in emergency settings. In one instance, a middle-aged man was brought to UPMC urgent care in an unconscious state. After identification was found in his wallet, the attending physician used the solution to view the man's medical record and discovered that the individual had chronic liver failure, in addition to secondary issues including hepatitis C. The doctor quickly determined the patient was in a hepatic coma and prescribed medication to lower the patient's life-threatening ammonia level.

The solution integrates patient information from across the UPMC network—such as from inpatient, outpatient, and physician's offices—and consolidates that data onto a single medical record. With immediate access to meaningful and comprehensive data, such as test results, physicians can dispense treatments more effectively, and patients are subject to less duplicate testing, thereby reducing pain and unnecessary expenses.

Doctors can also diagnose conditions more easily. For instance, in one case, medication information from one clinic prevented another clinic from prescribing a different drug, thereby preventing a potential drug-drug interaction. The information also revealed patient narcotics abuse. In another instance, allergy information prevented serious medical consequences that a patient could have experienced during testing and treatment of a disease. The solution also provides caregivers with information about known infectious diseases, enabling them to take the necessary precautions to protect themselves and other patients.

Let us now move toward real-time analytics for the healthcare industry. A century ago, a new baby was just as much a cause for concern as a cause for joy, as more than one in 10 infants died at birth or shortly thereafter. While that number has dropped significantly, the number of premature births (7.1 percent) may actually be on the rise in Canada. These early births are responsible for 75 percent of all infant deaths in Canada. Even when infants survive, premature babies may develop lifelong problems unless cared for properly. Although state-of-the-art medical devices monitor premature babies, neonatologists are increasingly burdened by vast quantities of charted data and many false alarms from medical devices. Neonates represent the second major cohort (other than patients over 62 years of age) for intensive care unit (ICU) admissions.

IBM and the University of Ontario Institute of Technology (UOIT) worked on an innovative research project to help doctors detect subtle changes in the condition of critically ill premature babies. The project involved a group of internationally recognized researchers, led by Dr. Carolyn McGregor, a UOIT associate professor and Canada Research Chair in Health Informatics. They used advanced stream computing software developed by IBM Research to greatly enhance the decision-making capabilities of doctors. The software ingests a constant stream of biomedical data, such as heart rate and respiration, along with environmental data gathered from advanced sensors and more traditional monitoring equipment on and around the babies. The researchers also used the software to apply findings from Dr. McGregor's body of research to help make "sense" of the data and, in near real-time, feed the resulting analysis to health-care professionals so they can predict potential changes in an infant's condition with greater accuracy and can intervene more quickly.

Physicians in neonatal intensive care units (NICUs) at Toronto's Hospital for Sick Children and two other international hospitals participated in the study. Monitoring "preemies" as a patient group is especially important because certain life-threatening conditions, such as infection, can be detected up to 24 hours in advance by observing changes in physiological data streams. Currently, physicians monitoring preemies rely on a paper-based process that involves manually looking at the readings from various monitors and getting feedback from the nurses providing care. "Right now, there is an enormous amount of critical data produced by machines monitoring patients," says Don Aldridge, business executive for IBM research and life science. "That creates a challenge. The ability to quickly analyze that data and make informed decisions will help improve the overall quality of health care."[6]

"Building upon our work in Canada and Australia, we will apply our research to premature babies at hospitals in China. With this new additional data, we can compare the differences and similarities of diverse populations of premature babies across continents," says Dr. McGregor. "In comparing populations, we can set the rules to optimize the system to alert us when symptoms occur in real-time, which is why having the streaming capability that the IBM platform offers is critical. The types of complexities that we're looking for in patient populations would not be accessible with traditional relational database or analytical approaches."[7]

Dr. McGregor's contributions include: 1) the first On-Demand Virtual NICUs Supporting Rural, Remote, and Urban Neonatal Care, 2) new approaches to data mining to support null hypothesis–based clinical research that can predict the onset of critical medical conditions, and 3) the real-time cross-correlation of physiological data to support predictors that allow the generation of complex neonatal medical alerts.[8]

Automobiles and Car Insurance

The next story in CEA involves cars and our experience as drivers. My guilt with wasting gas and global warming led to me purchasing an environment-friendly green car. Every time I drive the car, the car rates my performance on the "green" index. The more I overuse the car and waste energy, the more the car penalizes my performance with a low score. If I drive it more carefully, with a mind toward energy consumption, I am rewarded with the maximum score of 5. While the score is displayed just to me, it gives me economic value in terms of gas consumption, as well as car wear and tear. The experience is collected, collated, analyzed, and displayed.

Can we take this driving experience and do something more with it? How would you like your insurance company to monitor your driving every moment you're behind the wheel? It's already happening. Insurers are offering potential discounts to people who voluntarily install a device that tracks how their car is driven and streams the data back to the company. By matching a "good driver" profile, participants can reduce their insurance premiums by 10 to 50 percent.[9]

So far, we are talking about money saved, so we are happy as customers. However, can this data also be used by insurers and claim attorneys against us? Car insurance companies would like you to install a new device in your car so they could track how you drive and when you drive. "The companies say this could reduce your insurance rates, but there is more to the story," observed a *USA Today* editorial. The data the insurers collect might not stay just with the insurers, and it might not be used only to calculate rates. "Police could get access to your driving habits, as could state agencies. Most critically, these data could be used in claims disputes by the insurer and others against you. That means that the auto insurer's 'black box' in your car could become Exhibit A in a case against you. Collecting better data about accidents is important for auto safety, but fairness remains a critical concern if drivers are told they have to accept the determination of an insurance company."[10]

Maybe our cars can do more than monitor driving. How about using technology not only to collect driving data but also to provide supervisory control so the driver is given fewer options for bad behaviors? I might not like those options for myself, but it is a perfect choice for teenaged kids whose safety, cars, and driving behaviors are the responsibilities of their parents.

Rajit Johri is currently working on a Ph.D. thesis at University of Michigan that designs a smart, self-learning Power Management Controller.[11,12] The goal is to design an intelligent supervisory controller that considers multiple objectives, such as fuel economy and low transient in-vehicle exhaust, with the end result of cleaner vehicles with smaller or no after-treatment systems. Efficient energy-source management provides additional degrees of freedom in engine operation, and the whole power train can be designed to improve desired performance criteria. The primary task is to maximize fuel economy, while ensuring safe operation regardless of the driver demand and vehicle states.

The gains with the hybrid vehicle are expected from effective regenerative braking and optimized engine operation. The probabilistic driver model is based on statistically sampling the driving habits of large numbers of drivers over different commutes. Using this model, the controller creates multiple future scenarios and chooses the command that in maximum likelihood will decrease the total trip cost. The whole vehicle is operated to give a pleasant driving experience to the driver, custom-suited to his or her liking with the added benefit of reduced fuel consumption and tailpipe emissions. This type of CEA application is very powerful because it incorporates a powerful analytics component to modify the operations. The analytics engine works in real-time, modifying the performance of the car engine, while its predictive component collects historical data for future adaptability of the car engine.

Retail

Now, let us move to retail and the consumer goods industry. Historically, advertisers paid newspapers to deliver grocery coupons. As cost-conscious consumers, we invested our precious time to accumulate coupons Sunday morning while reading newspapers. Assuming we remembered to carry the coupons with us, we went shopping in the afternoon at the grocery store. We handed the coupons to the clerk after shopping and received discounts. The process hardly ever worked for me. There were too many manual steps and many opportunities for me to forget. Only a small number of coupons actually resulted in real savings.

Now let us look at a different way of distributing coupons. The grocery store seeks my permission to deliver the coupons electronically to me every time I enter the grocery store, using Short Message Service (SMS) messages to my cell phone. Every time I enter the grocery store, the cell phone registers my presence, and the grocery store marketing system delivers coupons to my cell phone. When I reach the checkout counter, the amount is automatically deducted based on the coupons delivered and the products purchased by me.

While this scenario mentioned kills the advertising revenue for the Sunday newspaper, it gives me a much better way of working with my grocery store. I do not have to remember the coupons at each step of the way, and the store has a much less expensive delivery cost. The effectiveness is much higher, and the grocery store gets an A+ from me for customer experience. At the same time that this delivery method is convenient and cost-effective to the consumer, it also provides the consumer products industry with tremendous capabilities to personalize campaigns. By combining communications information from the telecommunications service provider with the shopping information from the retail industry, we now have a rich set of data about the consumer, and, under opt-in, this information can be used to customize and personalize the discount offers.

Information Services

In 2009, I decided to take my family for a vacation in Italy. I have been traveling to international destinations extensively for over three decades, and it takes me a month each time to plan the vacation. My usual process of searching for the best places to visit and restaurants to eat was based on AAA brochures. As the Internet gave me the flexibility to search destinations online, I mechanized my searches, without significantly changing the process. I scoured the Internet looking for brochures, read their descriptions, and guessed which restaurants would be closest to our liking. My daughter had a different idea. She went through sites like Yelp and TripAdvisor and sought help from her friends (online, obviously) to find rare places that were both inexpensive and delicious. We ate almost like locals in Rome and Florence, and by throwing a couple of Italian phrases into the mix, we almost acted like ones too.

As I was introduced to Yelp, I started to use it more often for my restaurant searches. I realized the site has given customers the ultimate weapon. If you like a restaurant, you can give it a good rating. If the restaurant fails to provide good food or good service, you can give a bad rating and review to let the world know about it. This information is very real and very immediate. Yelp can even organize the rating historically to show the next viewer whether the restaurant is improving or worsening or has a loyal set of customers and occasional ranters.

Earlier, I mentioned using data from the communications industry to help retailers. We have another great example of communications data helping information services. In the past 20 years, we have seen the rapid proliferation of navigation devices for automobiles that use Global Positioning System (GPS) to map directions from one location to another. The navigation tools in the 1980s were primarily paper-based "trip tick" maps that charted a path using preprinted maps. The person assembling the maps often used information about construction and heavy rush-hour congestion to recommend alternate paths. As the early devices were introduced, they brought a level of automation that allowed us to dynamically re-chart the path based on current location. However, these early devices missed the human touch and often took us through busy routes and construction sites. The evolution has finally caught on with the human touch offered in the old days. If there is traffic congestion on the road, it leads to a lot of slow-moving travelers and a resulting unusual concentration of mobile signals. What if a mobile operator would take all the mobile signal data, remove personal information, and summarize the data in the form of heat maps—showing locations where mobile signal is unusually heavy, signifying a traffic jam?

TomTom is a provider of car navigation equipment. TomTom devices contain up-to-the-minute information from multiple data sources, including anonymous GPS measurements from personal navigation devices and mobile phone signals, road sensors, and journalistic data. Using proprietary and tested methods, TomTom dynamically merges this information and makes it available in real-time to customers in the personal navigation, cell phone, fleet management, government, and in-vehicle markets. When HD Traffic is added to a navigation solution, end users can be automatically rerouted around jams and potentially save time and money, minimize environmental impact, and enjoy a significantly improved navigation experience.

"You won't find a more accurate or reliable source of live traffic information anywhere," says Ralf-Peter Schäfer, Traffic Director of TomTom. "The live traffic map is the perfect starting point for anyone planning a journey or who needs the most up-to-date view of the traffic on the road. By giving more drivers access to TomTom HD Traffic, we hope that we can start to make better use of the road network and start to reduce traffic congestion for everyone."[13]

Conclusion

This chapter has provided a series of scenarios across a cross-section of industries to illustrate how CEA is helping us as consumers and supporting businesses in offering new and improved service. Here are a couple of general observations from the case studies.

The customer is the consumer of the service. The communications service providers refer to these people as "subscribers." The health care industry addresses them as "patients." Automobile manufacturers and car insurance companies deal with "drivers." The retail industry is supporting "shoppers."

In each case, there is a need to understand key attributes of the customer and rationalize across diverse sources to correlate data for a customer.

These case studies show a rapid increase in velocity and volume of data. The sensors, whether NICU data on heart rate or mobile signal data for navigation devices, is being generated automatically and requires a response in real-time or near real-time. In all of these cases, if the analytics solution requires an hour to collect, collate, mine, and act upon the data, it may significantly reduce the value to the customer. The solution must act in real-time or near real-time.

At the same time, the case studies show significant intelligence in developing insight about these customers. The insight comes from algorithms that may take hours or days to execute on the historical data. We have mastered our capabilities for combining real-time analytics, which is very fast, with predictive modeling, which is very deep.

The trend is towards cross-industry correlation. Data about credit scores, shopping habits, communications signals, and social networking is being used by other industries, which use the core data to build customer insights. This data is being packaged and sold using a sophisticated information services market that has placed a monetary value on customer data and a market exchange where consumer data can be traded across businesses.

These case studies are rapidly changing the competitive landscape across a number of industries, seriously questioning the status quo and offering new products and business models. As we develop the business proposition and CEA solution in this book, I will be mapping how CEA supports these case studies. Irrespective of the industry you are dealing with, CEA is a vital tool for creating a disruptive business model that radically redefines how we serve our customers.

CHAPTER 2

Instrumentation and Automation Fuels Customer Experience Data Collection

In Chapter 1, I used a series of case studies to explore practices in Customer Experience Analytics. These scenarios identified a range of capabilities for CEA covering a number of industries. Large automation investments in customer touch points, products, and business processes are rapidly creating enormous volumes of data as well as capabilities to make changes at electronic speeds. This section explores these changes in "instrumentation" and how that provides an environment for CEA.

IVR, kiosks, mobile devices, email, chat, corporate web sites, third-party applications, and social networks have generated a fair amount of event information about the customers. In addition, customer interaction via traditional media, such as call centers, can now be analyzed and organized. The biggest change is in our ability to modify the customer experience using software —policies, procedures, and personalization—making self-service increasingly customer-friendly.

This chapter covers the data and levers for customer experience across functional areas. The availability of raw data about the customers provides us with an unprecedented opportunity not only to analyze and understand the customer but also to adaptively change customer-facing systems and processes to improve customer experience.

Sales and Marketing

Let us start with customer shopping. Analytics related to customers and their experiences has been a widely studied area for over 50 years. Most of the core marketing science and related disciplines developed models of customer behavior, devised ways to measure customer experience, and used analytics to peek into the decision-making process. While academics worked on very impressive customer models and techniques for analysis and prediction, it was often difficult to apply these principles in practice, because of a lack of and high cost of data collection.

For example, when I was working on my Ph.D. thesis, I worked with Professor Robert Meyer to study consumer buyer behavior and help develop a mathematical model.[14] The model used a grocery-store learning game. While it was theoretically possible to create a grocery-store learning model in a game setting, it was impossible to replicate the instrumentation in real life. The good news is that all the work in marketing science can now be applied as the data becomes available. To their definition, I would like to add the tasks associated with data ingestion, categorization, and management to support the analytics.

Sales and marketing got their biggest boost in instrumentation from the Internet-driven automation over the past 10 years. Browsing, shopping, ordering, and customer service on the Web has not only provided tremendous control to end users; it has also created an enormous flood of information to the marketing, product, and sales organization in understanding buyer behavior. Each sequence of web clicks can be collected, collated, and analyzed for customer delight, puzzlement, dysphoria, or outright defection and the sequence leading to this decision.

Self-service has crept in through a variety of means: IVRs, kiosks, handheld devices, and many others. Each of these electronic means of communication act like a gigantic pool of time-and-motion studies. We have data available on how many steps a customer took, how many products she compared, and what she focused on: price, features, brand comparisons, recommendations, defects, and so on. Suppliers have gained enormous amounts of data from self-service, electronic leashes connected to products, and the use of IT. If I use a two-way set-top box to watch television, the supplier has instant access to my channel-surfing behavior. Did I change the channel when the advertisement started? Did I turn the volume up or down when the jingle started to play? If I use the Internet to shop for a product, my click stream can be analyzed and used to study shopping behavior. How many products did I look at? What did I view in each product? Was it the product description or the price? This enriched set of data allows us to analyze customer experience in the minutest detail.

What are the sources of data from such self-service interactions?

- *Product*—As products become increasingly electronic, they provide a lot of valuable data to the supplier regarding product use and product quality. In many cases, suppliers can also collect information about the context in which a product was used. Products can also supply information related to frequency of use, interruptions, usage skipping, and other related aspects.
- *Electronic touch points*—A fair amount of data can be collected from the touch points used for product shopping, purchase, use, or payment. IVR tree traversals can be logged, web click streams can be collected, and so on.
- *Components*—Sometimes, components may provide additional information. This information could include data about component failures, use, or lack thereof. For example, a wireless telecommunications provider can collect data from networks, cell towers, third parties, and handheld devices to understand how all the components together provided a good or bad service to the customer.

As much as we have used instrumentation to collect rich amounts of customer data, CEA can also be used to drive a new set of behaviors. Over the past 30 years, we have seen gradual maturing of our understanding of CEA and how it impacts sales and marketing. The early evolution was in use of CEA for segmentation. The original segmentations were demographic in nature and used hard consumer data—such as geography, age, gender, and ethnic characteristics—to establish market segmentations. Marketers soon realized that behavioral traits were important parameters to segment the customers.

As our understanding grew, we saw more emphasis on micro segments— specific niche markets based on CEA-driven parameters. For example, marketers started to differentiate innovators and early adapters, as compared with late adapters, in their willingness to purchase new electronic gadgets. Customer experience data let us characterize innovators who were eager to share experiences and were more tolerant of product defects.

In the mid-1990s, with automation in customer touch points and use of the Internet for customer self-service, marketing started to get interested in personalization and 1:1 marketing. As Martha Rogers and Don Peppers point out in their book *The One to One Future*, "The basis for 1:1 marketing is share of customer, not just market share. Instead of selling as many products as possible over the next sales period to whomever will buy them, the goal of the 1:1 marketer is to sell one customer at a time as many products as possible over the lifetime of that customer's patronage. Mass marketers develop a product and try to find customers for that product. But 1:1 marketers develop a customer and try to find products for that customer."[15]

Early CEA systems were reporting systems that provided raw segmentation data to the marketing team so that they could use the data to decide on marketing activities, such as campaigns. Automation in marketing and operations gave us the opportunity to close the loop—use CEA to collect effectiveness data to revise and improve campaigns. We are seeing surges in campaign activity. Marketers are interested in micro-campaigns that are designed specifically for a micro-segment or, in some cases, for specific customers. The customer experience information gives us criteria for including a customer in the campaign.

For example, prepaid wireless providers are engaging in micro-campaigns targeted at customers who are about to run out of their prepaid minutes. These customers are the most likely to churn to a competitor and could easily continue with their current wireless provider if they were to be directed to a store that sells prepaid wireless cards.

Another area of interest is Next Best Action (NBA)—in other words, recommending an activity based on the customer's latest experience with the product. This could include an up-sell/cross-sell based on current product ownership, usage level, and behavioral profile. NBA could be offered any time the sales organization has the opportunity to connect with the customer via a touch point. NBA is far more effective in sales conversion compared with canned rules that repeatedly offer the same product over and over across a customer interaction channel. (Imagine your airline offering you a discounted trip to your favorite warm-weather golf vacation spot on a cold day.) NBA can also be revised based on feedback from customer reaction.

Pricing has been a hotly pursued topic for business, as each percent increase in price without a corresponding decrease in demand means an increase in profits. There has been a growing trend to use price optimization models— mathematical programs that calculate how demand varies at different price levels—and then combine that data with information about costs and inventory levels to recommend prices that will improve profits. Given the complexity of pricing and the thousands of items in highly dynamic market conditions, modeling results and insights helps to forecast demand, develop pricing and promotional strategies, control inventory levels, and improve customer satisfaction.[16]

Operations

In a typical operation, automation leads to an opportunity to collect customer data that can be used for analytics. For example, in the health care case study in the preceding chapter, we studied Neonatal Intensive Care Units that collected vital statistics from babies and either alerted the medical staff or took corrective actions based on patient data. In this case, the task of routine monitoring was automated, thereby freeing up the staff time to treatment. The automation provided the opportunity to record all the vitals in an electronic form that can be not only monitored but also collated and analyzed for trends and predictive modeling.

How do we use operational data to improve customer experience? Let us take an insurance example. If we collect enough operational data about the customers, we should be able to measure their health. The obvious impact is in insurance underwriting. Deloitte consulting has developed a predictive model for life insurance[17] that provides a significant reduction in operational cost for life insurance policy evaluation using CEA. The rough sequence is that the insurer receives an application, and then a predictive model score is calculated and a policy is either offered or sent through traditional underwriting. The predictive model is typically used, not to make the underwriting decisions, but rather to triage applications and suggest whether additional requirements are needed before making an offer. To that end, the model takes in information from any source that is available in near real-time for a given applicant. This can include third-party marketing data and more traditional underwriting data. Compared with a traditional underwriting, the predictive model allows an underwriter to skip routine tests for a "healthy customer," leading to a cost saving of $125 per applicant while at the same time improving the customer experience (Table 2.1).

Table 2.1: Illustrative underwriting savings from predictive model requirement cost			
Data source	Traditional underwriting	Requirement Utilization	Predictive Model
Paramedical exam	$55	50%	0%
Oral fluids analysis	$25	20%	0%
Blood and urine Analysis	$55	70%	0%
MVR report	$6	70%	75%
Attending physician statement	$100	20%	0%
Medical exam	$120	20%	0%
EKG	$75	10%	0%
Stress test	$450	1%	0%
Third-party data	$0.50	0%	100%
Total cost per applicant		$130	$5
Savings per applicant		$125	

Product Engineering

Products are increasingly run by the electrons, giving us an enormous opportunity to measure customer experience. We take photos digitally and then post them on Facebook, providing an opportunity to do face recognition without requiring laborious cycles in digitization. We listen to songs on Pandora on the Internet, creating an opportunity to measure what we like or dislike, or how often we skip a song after listening to the part of it we like the most. We read books electronically on the Internet or on our favorite handheld devices, giving publishers an opportunity to understand what we read and how many times. We watch television using a two-way set-top box that can record each channel click and correlate it to analyze whether the channel was switched right before, during, or right after the commercial break. Even mechanical products, such as automobiles, are offering an increasing number of ways to interact with them electronically. We make all our ordering transactions electronically, giving third parties opportunities to analyze our spending habits, by month, by season, by ZIP+4 and by tens of thousands of micro-segments. Usage data can be synthesized to study the quality of customer experience and can be mined for component defects, successes, or extensions. This data can also be used by marketing to understand micro-segmentation. In a wireless company, we isolated problems in the use of cell phones to defective device antenna by analyzing call quality and comparing them across devices.

Products can be test marketed and changed based on feedback. They can also be customized and personalized for every consumer or micro-segment based on their needs. CEA plays a major role in customizing, personalizing, and changing products based on customer feedback. Product engineering combines a set of independent components into a product in response to a customer need. Component quality impacts overall product performance. Can we use CEA data to isolate badly performing components and replace them with good ones? In addition, can we simplify the overall product by removing components that are rarely used and offer no real value to the customer? A lot of product engineering analytics using customer experience data can lead to building simplified products that best meet customer requirements.

To conduct this analysis and predictive modeling, we need a good understanding of components used and how they participate in the customer experience. Once a good amount of data is collected, the model can be used to isolate badly performing components by isolating the observations from customer experience and tracing them to the badly performing component. Complex products, such as automobiles, telecommunications networks, and engineering goods benefit from this type of analytics around product engineering.

Finance

Chief financial officers (CFOs) are interested in reducing revenue leakage, closely tying revenues to actual product usage and looking for ways to plug pilferage or fraud. Fraud detection is a classic example of CEA's applications to finance.

CEA is used to more accurately compute the overall risk for a customer. The customer may be an individual or a family. Each family member may have one or many accounts with a bank. An account may result in the bank assuming a risk associated with the transactions. By identifying the overall household relationships and all the risks associated with the household, the bank accurately assesses the overall risk. A tremendous amount of public records and credit rating information is available on each member of the household. In addition to the bank records, external data provides data about the relationships the household has with other banks.

How much outside data can we use to compute risks? For example, a life insurance company can purchase location data from a communications service provider, commerce data from the order analytics marketplace (which is in its embryonic stage), and social data from Facebook to compute a health risk index, differentiating junk food addict from fitness crazy person. Can it use this data to offer different risk premiums for life insurance? How about using health insurance transactions to assess life insurance candidacy and risk?

Fraud detection and prevention is another important financial application of CEA data. Predictive models combined with real-time information on location, credit-card transactions, types of calls made, and so on can be used to detect fraudulent use of credit cards, phones, or other products.

Across the Customer Life Cycle

Product managers often study the customer life cycle to explore ways to excel in customer experience. A customer life cycle starts when a customer starts shopping for a product and leans on all available sources for product evaluations. Once the customer decides on the product, he or she proceeds to buy the product and starts using the product. Depending on the use and associated problems, there may be a need for customer service, which results in the customer either becoming an advocate and buying more or becoming dissatisfied. Analytics plays a major role in the customer life cycle in understanding shopping criteria, how customers collect information, how they perceive the ordering experience, what they think of product quality during installation and use, and how they obtain customer service or pay for the product. It provides key insights to improve customer experience across the customer life cycle (see Figure 2.1).

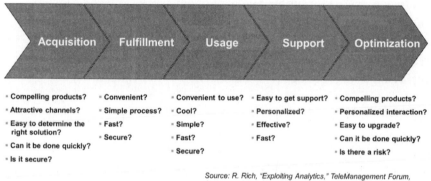

Source: R. Rich, "Exploiting Analytics," TeleManagement Forum, September 2010, http://www.tmforum.org.

Figure 2:1: Customer life cycle

Conclusions

CEA is based on available customer experience data. This includes customer demographics, psychographics, usage information, customer service experience, payment record, troubleshooting, and sharing of experience. Given the level of automation in customer-facing business processes, a tremendous amount of information is available regarding customer experience. It includes unstructured information, such as blog postings, Twitter feeds, and product reviews, as well as structured information, such as payment, product quality, trouble data, and everything in between.

The Internet has provided worldwide access to every consumer, which is critical when new products are introduced and face customer reviews shared across third-party sites. Sensors provide a lot of data about customer actions, some of which may be duplicated and would require synthesis or harmonization. However, most of this data is fragmented, often duplicated, and full of errors. A critical part of CEA is the collation and synthesis of the data. As we saw in the telecom and healthcare examples in Chapter 1, this may provide us with powerful capabilities for real-time monitoring of customer experience.

A key component of CEA lies in synthesizing historical customer experience data into a set of models. These models represent customer experience and related actions. They predict conditions under which a customer would churn. They provide criteria for further purchase or advocacy to other customers. These models can then be applied during customer experience to score alternatives and provide the "next best action." Depending on the level of sophistication, models could be built by analysts or software and applied via manual changes in processes or automatically inserted into the actions.

The analytics results in certain actions, whether changes to customer policies, business processes, or specific actions inserted during the next customer interaction. The actions may involve changes to the product themselves or to their prices. It may include how many or which channels may be used to sell or serve to the customers. It may include payment platforms. We might use analytics to segment customers and provide different products, prices, promotions, or service depending on customer segment. Models can also be used to understand the location at which a customer is most likely to buy a product, whether physical or virtual. In many cases, policies regarding how we deal with customers play an important role in customer satisfaction, and these policies may be fine-tuned based on profitability and customer satisfaction. For example, providing a refund or discount for poor quality may result in increased customer satisfaction but reduce margins. Analytics can help understand the policy that provides the best balance between the two objectives.

The end result as seen by the customer is a change in product or service. This change must be done while the customer is interacting with the product or a customer touch point. In the past, analytics was used to study customer reactions and make changes in price, product, or promotions with a long lead time between customer reaction and change in product or price. Increasingly, we are seeing adaptive products, prices, or service policies that are changed rapidly in response to customer reaction. For example, a new product introduction may lead to a positive or negative customer sentiment. This sentiment may be captured from third-party blogs and used rapidly to change either the product or associated messaging during the product launch, and this could even be done the same day the blogs were posted!

The inputs include:

- *Customer data*—This includes customer demographics, psychographics, and customer hierarchy/relationships, such as householding. We can segment customers based on where they live, what they like to do, and what they have done historically. Customer data includes third-party information collected, collated, and sold to information consumers.
- *Location data*—Customer location is the most widely debated topic at the time of the writing of this book in the summer of 2011. The presence of smart devices connected to wireless networks have provided a tremendous amount of customer data that can be used (with permission or in a summarized manner) for a variety of applications.
- *Usage/Event data*—Information about product use is typically created through event and alarm generation from the product. We saw a variety of industry-specific data obtained from network (communications service providers), driving behavior (automotive), physiological information (health care), and so on.
- *Payment data*—Information about purchase and payments.
- *Social network data*—Data available from social networking sites, Facebook, Yelp, Twitter, and so on.
- *Other third-party data*—Any other third-party data available for purchase, such as credit rating, location, addresses, and so on.

CHAPTER 3

Rise in Customer Sophistication

As I watch my two kids grow, I feel envious of how they make their decisions today compared with what I did 35 years ago. The increase in information level and the associated tooling has created a new breed of sophisticated consumers. These consumers are far more analytic, far savvier at using statistics, and far more connected using a social media to rapidly collect and collate opinion from others.

This chapter will focus on understanding how this customer sophistication is manifesting in their product shopping, evaluations, use, and sharing of information among circle of influence. This includes how they collect and organize product information, view the product or the supplier, and how they measure and evaluate which product to buy, use, or recommend. Note that this analysis has been done from the perspective of the business-to-consumer market. The business-to-business market has additional framework components that we will not address here.

Evolution of Consumer Decision-Making Process

We live a world full of marketing messages. While most of the marketing is still broadcast using newspaper, magazine, network TV, radio, and display advertising, even in the conventional media, narrow casting is gradually finding its way—local advertisement insertions in magazines, insertion of narrow cast commercials using set-top boxes, and use of crowd information to change display ads. The Internet world, on the other hand, is highly personalized. Search engines, social network sites, and electronic yellow pages are inserting advertisements specific to an individual or to a micro-segment. Internet cookies are increasingly used to track user behavior and for tailoring content based on user behavior.

To quote a 2009 article published in the *McKinsey Quarterly*: "Consumers are moving outside the purchasing funnel—changing the way they research and buy your products. If your marketing has not changed in response, it should. In today's decision journey, consumer-driven marketing is increasingly important as customers seize control of the process and actively pull information helpful to them. Our research found that two-thirds of the touch points during the active-evaluation phase involve consumer-driven marketing activities, such as Internet reviews and word-of-mouth recommendations from friends and family, as well as in-store interactions and recollections of past experiences. A third of the touch points involve company-driven marketing. Traditional marketing remains important, but the changes in the way consumers make decisions means that marketers must move aggressively beyond purely push-style communication and learn to influence consumer-driven touch points, such as word-of-mouth and Internet information sites."[18]

Email and text messages rapidly brought us closer to interpersonal interactions. The communication started not only with marketers but also with third parties and friends. This was followed by bulletin boards, group chats, and social media, giving us the ability to converse about our purchase intentions, fears, expectations, and disappointments with small and large social groups. Unlike email and text, the conversations are on the Web for others to read, now or later.

So far, we are dealing with single forms of communication. The next sets of sources combine information from more than one media. As I shopped at an electronics store for a navigation device, the salesperson logged into Amazon to show me that the prices quoted by him were below the prices on the Amazon site. We can use smart phones to collect information in a store about the product features, prices, comparisons, and more. Second world and alternate reality are becoming interesting avenues for trying out product ideas in a make-believe world where product usage can be experimented with.

We often need experts to help us sort out product features and how they relate to our product usage. A large variety of experts are available today to help us with usage, quality, pricing, and value-related information about products. Sometimes, these experts are truly independent of the marketers, but often the experts are paid by the marketers, bringing into question their objectivity. So, then we can have experts on experts—trade journals and consumer advisory groups that can tell us whether an expert is unbiased.

At the end of the day, we are swayed far more by people we know and trust. This is the biggest contribution of social networks. They have brought consumers together such that sharing of customer experience is now far more frequent than ever before.

While there may be myriads of ways to evaluate a product, there are three major categories of evaluation:

- *Economics*—How the product meets the need and provides utility to the consumer. This is the most studied topic for economists. A product is considered valuable if its perceived utility is higher than its price.
- *Psychographics*—Covers aspects not easily justifiable by economics. I may pay an enormous amount of money for a sports car because it is able to accelerate quickly, although it may provide the same utility as a much less expensive car. The acceleration may not be justifiable via time savings and may result in additional traffic tickets.
- *Sociographics*—How my social network views the product. Is it in fashion? Is it considered trendy? Does it have a high quality in my social network?

Consumers use a combination of economics, psychographics, and sociographics to evaluate a product. If there are many choices, most of us rule out most of the candidates by eliminating them by attribute and conduct a rigorous comparison among only the top two or three alternatives. The evaluation process begins even before a consumer starts shopping for a product. Even if we have not actively evaluated or shopped, we have opinions about products. The criteria and their weights change rapidly after we purchase a product. Once we start loving a product, we begin recommending it to others. Also, we are influenced by others and their opinions.

Depending on our personality, we might be very analytical and use formal models to evaluate a product. On the other hand, we might be very impulsive or subjective in evaluating products. Irrespective of the formality used for evaluation, our opinions and desires impact product purchase, use, and price elasticity. We are very willing to pay a very high margin for a cup of coffee at Starbucks but may be supersensitive to price while shopping for airline tickets.

Use of Social Networks

Social networks have enabled groups of consumers to share product evaluations. As of July 30, 2011, Facebook has over 706 million users, of whom about 21 percent are in the United States.[19] Recommendations by personal acquaintances and opinions posted by consumers online are the most trusted forms of advertising globally, according to the 2009 Nielsen Global Online Consumer Survey of over 25,000 Internet consumers from 50 countries.[20] There are many ways to utilize social networks to influence purchase and reuse:

- *Studying consumer experience*—A fair amount of this data is unstructured. By analyzing the text for sentiments, intensity, readership, related blogs, referrals, and other information, we can organize the data into positive and negative influences and their impact on the customer base.
- *Organizing customer experience*—Providing the reviews to a prospective buyer, so they can gauge how others evaluated the product.
- *Influencing social networks*—Providing marketing material, product changes, company directions, and celebrity endorsements to the social networks, so that the buzz may be injected and enhanced by the social media.
- *Feedback to products, operations, or marketing*—Using information generated by social media to rapidly make changes in the product mix and marketing to improve the offering to the customer base.

Society has always played a major role in our evaluation process. However, the Internet and social networking have radically altered our access to information. I may choose to "like" a product on a social network site, and my network now has instant access to this action. If I consider a restaurant worth its money, Yelp can help me broadcast that fact worldwide. If I hate the new cell phone service from a telecommunications service provider, I can blog to complain about it to everyone.

Role of Leaders in Product Selection and Churn

In any group, there are leaders. These are the people who lead a change from one brand to another. Leaders typically have a set of followers. Once a leader switches a brand, it increases the likelihood for the social group members to churn as well. Who are these leaders? Can we identify them? How can we direct our marketing to these leaders?

In any communication, the leaders are always the center of the hub (see Figure 3.1). They are often connected to a larger number of "followers," some of whom could also be leaders. In the figure, the leaders have a lot more communication arrows either originating or terminating to them compared with others.

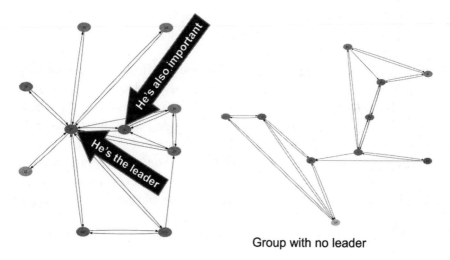

Group with no leader

Figure 3.1: Leaders in a communications network

How do we identify the leaders? IBM Research conducted a series of experiments with communications service providers.[21] The input to the analysis was the Call Detail Records (CDRs), which carry information about person A calling person B. By synthesizing call information and abstracting communications network, we discovered the web of communications across individuals. We also used the customer churn information to correlate churn among the leaders to subsequent churn among followers. Here are some of the highlights from one of the experiments I helped conduct:

- Leaders are 1.2 times more likely to churn compared with non-leaders.
- There are two types of leaders: disseminating leaders and authority leaders. The former are closely connected to their group using outgoing calls, while the latter are connected through a larger proportion of incoming calls.
- When a disseminating leader churned, additional churns were 28.5 times more likely. When an authority leader left the group, additional churns were 19.9 times more likely.
- Typically, there is a very limited time between leaders' churn and the churn of the followers.

The social groups can be inferred in any type of communication—emails, SMS text, calls, Facebook friends, and so on. It is interesting to see strong statistics associated with leaders' influence on the group.

The past 10 years have seen a massive explosion in the amount of data available about customer experience and the types of changes in the product mix. The leaders have been able to embrace the change and exploit it to their competitive advantage. CEA in this rapidly changing environment requires strong tools for data collection, data synthesis, monitoring, analysis, and modeling. Over the next couple of chapters, I will outline how businesses view customer experience and how its impact on business is measured and prioritized to develop an information management and analytics road map.

4

Rise of the CEA Marketplace

Today, there are many markets for CEA information exchange and for collaborative marketing to the customers. The data market is the primary example. The rise of the Internet coincided with a rise in free services. We can search information on the Web free of charge. We can find a restaurant in a new town without paying for a subscription. We can get email, watch videos, enjoy TV programs, find friends, obtain travel advice, and more. Equally interesting is the market for loyalty points. Airlines have teamed up with credit-card operators and a variety of other travel industries to reward customers for repeat purchases. The loyalty points are now being embraced by a variety of industries. How do these markets work? These developments raise severe privacy concerns and other regulatory issues. This chapter examines the CEA marketplace, how it is used, and how it is regulated.

The Data Bazaar

From a CEA perspective, the rise of the "data bazaar" is the biggest enabler to create an external marketplace where we can collect, exchange, and sell customer information. We are seeing a new trend in the marketplace, in which customer experience from one industry is anonymized, packaged, and sold to other industries. Fortunately for us, Internet advertising came to our rescue in providing an incentive to customers through free services and across-the-board opt-ins.

Internet advertising is a remarkably complex field. With over $26 billion in 2010 revenue[22], the industry is feeding a fair amount of startup and initial public offering (IPO) activity. What is interesting is that this advertising money is enhancing customer experience. Take the case of Yelp, which lets consumers share their experiences regarding restaurants, shopping, nightlife, beauty spas, active life, coffee and tea, and others.[23] Yelp obtains its revenues from advertising on its web site; however, most of the traffic is from people who access Yelp to read customer experience posted by others. With all this traffic coming to the Internet, the questions that arise are how is this Internet usage experience captured and packaged, and how are advertisements traded among advertisers and publishers.

CEA is creating a new market, where customer data from one industry can be collected, categorized, anonymized, and repackaged for sale to others:

- *Location*—As we discussed in Chapter 2, location is increasingly available to suppliers. Assuming a product is consumed using or in conjunction with a mobile device, the location of the consumer is an important piece of information that may be available to the supplier.
- *Cookies*—Web browsers carry enormous information using web cookies. Some of this may be directly associated with touch points.
- *Usage data*—A number of data providers have started to collect, synthesize, categorize, and package information for reuse. This includes credit-card agencies for credit-rating information, web browsers for cookie information, social networks for blogs published or "like" buttons clicked, and telecommunications organizations for location information. Some of this data may be available only in summary form or anonymized for the protection of customer privacy. Even summaries may be available at the micro-segment level, such as ZIP+4 in the United States.

"Terence Kawaja has a new way for potential investors to visualize it," says *Wall Street Journal* writer Amir Efrati. "The market involves hundreds of small and large companies that help advertisers reach consumers and help web site publishers, mobile-application developers, search engines, and other digital destinations generate revenue through advertising. Kawaja, who runs boutique investment firm LUMA Partners, spent months putting together six new graphics that show how 1,240 different companies fit into the following categories of online advertising: display, video, search engines, mobile, social, and commerce."[24] I have replicated Kawaja's Mobile Advertising LUMA Scape in Figure 4.1. For the rest of the LUMA Scapes, visit Kawaja's web site: *www.lumapartners.com*. A number of intermediaries play key roles in developing an advertising inventory, auction of the inventory to the ad servers, and the related payment process, as the advertisements are clicked and related buying decisions are tracked.

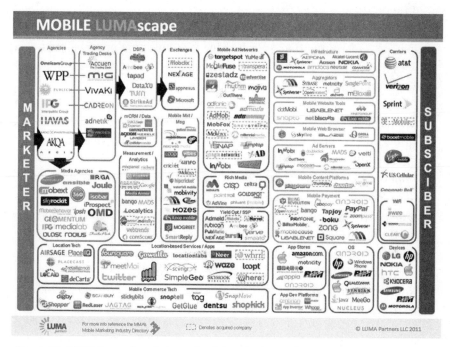

Figure 4.1: LUMA Scape for wireless advertising (reprinted with permission)

The Loyalty Marketplace

The airline industry was the first to embrace loyalty points in a big way to reward customers. They not only provided loyalty points for frequent flyers but also extended these points to business partners—hotels, car rental, credit card companies, and others. The loyalty programs have provided a strong business driver for understanding the single view of the customer (not only for an enterprise but often for the entire ecosystem, as in Star Alliance run by United and other airlines), rewarding customers for repeat buying and higher usage and thereby creating a bond that is hard to break. Feedback does not need to be monetary exchange. For example, my very green Honda Insight hybrid car indicates a rating on the eco-friendliness of my driving. The simplest way in which many organizations provide feedback is by personalizing the touch point when the customer registers with the web site.

How does feedback and reward impact the customer experience? Rewards can be used for:

- *Pricing and discounting*—High-value customers are provided with waivers on fees, cash and points, or points-based products and higher access to limited products (no blackout dates).
- *Product*—New products are often introduced first and exclusively to the loyal customers.
- *Touch points*—The experience is personalized for known customers, thereby letting an organization track usage.
- *Policy changes*—Loyal customers are given preferential treatment at the touch points, as well as a different set of rules for changes.
- *Usage*—Loyal customers are offered higher loyalty points for increased usage, for example double or triple points for selected promotions.
- *Location*—Premium customers are offered different queues, more accessibility to live agents, and higher service.
- *Resources*—Loyal customers get first access to higher-value resources—aisle seats, first class, economy plus, airline lounge access, and so on.

Auction Marketplace

Pricing has been a hotly pursued topic for business, as every percent increase in price without a corresponding demand decrease means an increase in profits. However, over the past decade, we have seen a new, dynamic pricing equilibrium favoring the customers and fueled by third-party pricing search tools. A typical third party, such as Travelocity or Priceline, offers customers the ability to search across an entire market and find deals. Ebay and other auction marketplaces have brought buyers and sellers together where price is determined through a bidding process. Wherever the product is perishable—

theater tickets or airline seats, for example—the new marketplace lets buyers find deals for items that need to move off the inventory or remain unsold.

This creates an interesting dynamic in that the suppliers are using sophisticated price optimization models to determine price based on supply and demand, and consumers are using third parties to find the best deals. Prices change often, with constant fine-tuning based on supply and demand. It is also bringing a new set of retailers who provide a layer of customer interface between the customer and the supplier. The retailer and the supplier now share responsibility for the customer experience, and they each have a direct impact on the resulting customer experience as felt at the end by the customer. After years of dealing with my favorite rental car company and receiving excellent differentiated service, I used a retailer and ended up purchasing a package including travel, hotel, and car rental, only to find that the premium customer policy for car rental cancellation no longer applied to this bundled package.

Social Networking Market

Social networking is the biggest trend in the current times and is the closest thing to unionizing the customer. As this book was being written, Twitter was generating 1,200 tweets per second and 110 million tweets per day[25]. We go to a restaurant after searching on Yelp, discussing with friends on Twitter, and using Facebook to collect a group together. We then use Yelp to write reviews, which are then used by others in turn to decide where to eat. We find jobs using LinkedIn or Dice. We buy books after reading reviews, watch movies based on recommendations, and make car purchase decisions after analyzing the buzz. While there is so much information available about the products and services we decide to buy, customers—especially the new Facebook generation—are increasingly adept at finding, utilizing, and sharing this information. Social networks can make obscure companies household legends or bring corporate stalwarts to their knees and even lead to the downfall of the most powerful of dictators.

So, what is the bottom line? Customer experience is now a center-stage necessity for brand survival. Those of us who cite the difficulties and stay away from the joys and risks of CEA programs are bound to extinction. The future belongs to those who master customer experience by properly analyzing it and designing their organization to excel in customer experience.

Privacy Concerns: Location

In the summer of 2011, we witnessed a hot debate regarding use of location data for monetization as well as other commercial and government use. According to company executives, Google and Apple collect and store location information from personal computers as well as mobile devices—a disclosure that sheds new light on the scope of the data collected by tech companies. Apple gathers information from some Apple Macintosh computers connected to Wi-Fi networks, and Google collects data from Wi-Fi–connected computers that use Google Chrome browsers or search "toolbars"[26] (see Figure 4.2). Under certain opt-in conditions, the collection and storage of location information may be permissible. Also, some of the data could be made anonymous and used for statistical analysis. Two bills introduced in the U.S. House and Senate would limit how the government and private companies can use information about your location, the latest signs of growing concern among lawmakers. The bills are among multiple efforts in Washington to update digital-privacy laws, particularly as they relate to location.

One bill, by Democratic Senators Al Franken of Minnesota and Richard Blumenthal of Connecticut, would require companies such as Apple and Google, as well as the makers of applications that run on their devices, to obtain user consent before sharing information with outsiders about the location of a mobile device. At a hearing last month, Franken said he had "serious doubts" that cell phone users' privacy was being protected. He convened the hearing after security researchers and *The Wall Street Journal* disclosed how iPhones and Android devices leave trails of electronic breadcrumbs revealing where they have been. The *Journal* also reported last year that 47 of 101 popular smart phone apps transmitted location data to outside companies without users' knowledge.

The other bill, by Senator Ron Wyden (D., Ore.) and Representative Jason Chaffetz (R., Utah), would require law-enforcement agencies to obtain a warrant in order to track an individual's location through a mobile phone or a special tracking device. It follows a bill introduced recently by Senate

Judiciary Committee Chairman Patrick Leahy (D., Vt.) that would impose a similar requirement and also require law enforcement to obtain a search warrant in order to retrieve old emails stored on servers. The laws around when government can track someone's location are murky. One key law dates from 1986, before the widespread use of cellphones or global-positioning satellites. Several cases are making their way through the courts now.[27]

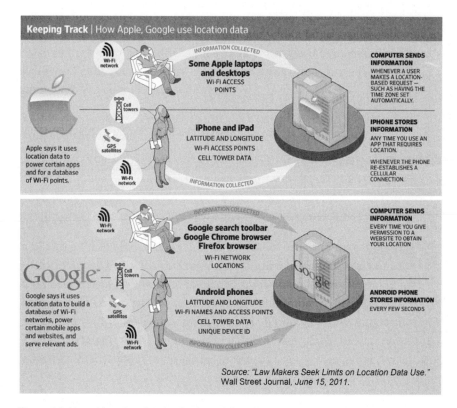

Figure 4.2: Use of location data by Apple and Google

Use of location data is a double-edged sword. On one hand, there are a large number of potential applications that help the consumers. For example, use of location data in an amusement park to locate lost children is a very positive customer experience. On the other hand, unauthorized use of location data by third parties is a potential bombshell that could lead to serious customer backlash. Any viable CEA solution that uses location data must be sensitive to the growing legal and customer concerns and the associated risks.

Summary

We have seen new markets emerge across the entire spectrum of CEA. Each of these markets has been disruptive. They have also created a mechanism to collect, trade, or sell customer information for everyone. There are significant geopolitical implications as well.

PART TWO:

The Customer Experience Analytics Solution

CHAPTER 5

Solution Overview

We have seen a number of forces that are driving the data generation, customer sophistication and availability of third-party sources for collecting, collating, and analyzing customer experience data. This explosion in the marketplace has brought a number of key requirements to the CEA architecture. The volumes have exploded. We are talking in terms of billions of transactions a day. The data includes structured and unstructured, text, photos, and videos. The sources could be inside or outside an organization, and all this has to be related to each other and make sense in real-time or near real-time to participate in the decision-making process for the consumers.

The CEA reference architecture provides a common architecture for a number of use cases described earlier. While the sources of data may be different, users may require different outputs, and the information stored in the information repository may vary, there are strong common themes that run across the reference architecture. Let me first highlight the five common differentiators that this architecture provides as compared with a typical business intelligence platform:

- *Massively parallel data integration and harmonization*—The data is coming from internal and external sources and includes batch and real-time sources. The data must be matched across these data sources to pinpoint on a specific customer. The data integration and harmonization component deals with collecting and harmonizing the data.

- *Stream computing*—A fair amount of data is sourced, correlated, synthesized, and analyzed in real-time (less than 100 milliseconds) or near real-time (less than 2 seconds), for example providing coupons on the phone as I enter the grocery store.
- *Predictive modeling*—The ability to analyze, model, and change the behavior of real-time analytics based on historical information and feedback from past actions. As a user reacts to an improved customer experience, the feedback regarding which service provider actions resulted in a positive reaction from the user are analyzed and used for modifications. For example, as certain policies result in improvement in customer satisfaction, those policies are incorporated into the customer services processes.
- *Analytics engine*—This is the historian that collects all the experience history and crunches the historical data to look for patterns using the commands provided by the predictive modeler. The engine must be able to store petabytes of data and retrieve or analyze the data against ad hoc queries.
- *Privacy management*—Privacy management is now a required component of a CEA architecture. It tracks information that customers have agreed to make public or selectively available to certain business partners. The rest of the sensitive information must be kept under lock and key to retain customers' trust.

Evolution

Customer Experience Analytics has evolved over three waves, as depicted in Figure 5.1.

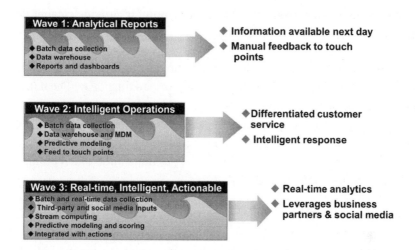

Figure 5.1: Implementation waves for Customer Experience Analytics

Wave 1 introduced analytical reporting in the 1990s. With the introduction of data warehouses and reporting, customer experience was one of the early areas for analytics, often triggered by marketing or call-center management. A typical data warehouse would collect customer contact or order information and would provide reports to analysts, who would in turn feed information to management. While Wave 1 created impressive gains in call-center performance and in customer segmentation, its progress was limited due to data quality and lack of Master Data Management.

Wave 2 introduced intelligence and was in response to some of the weaknesses of Wave 1 in the first decade of 2000. Single views of customer and product were the primary drivers and resulted in a single reporting master, with customer ID crisscrossing across various customer databases and providing basic data harmonization tools and processes for de-duplication. Wave 2 was also aided by the Sarbanes-Oxley Act in U.S. financial reporting, Basel III in the global financial sector, and HIPAA in the U.S. health sector, which provided increased regulations for cleaner customer information. However, much of the regulations were met with process improvements, with relatively lower emphasis on IT technology and tools. Wave 2 improved awareness for data quality and provided operational means for getting cleaner information for marketing and sales decision-making. Wave 2 also saw an unprecedented growth in web commerce and used that momentum to provide cleaner data for self-service.

Wave 3 is part of the current technological movement, in which social media and external data sources are taking a lead in organizing CEA. The data has exploded in size and velocity and has resulted in a lot more emphasis on real-time analytics, parallel processing, and predictive modeling to support real-time analytics. Wave 3 is providing a lot more actionable decisions, often embedded in customer-facing processes or communication touch points, including web interactions and SMS.

The primary technical challenge in implementing Wave 3 is our ability to integrate the batch model of Wave 2 with the real-time environment of Wave 3. The target architecture defined below is an attempt at showing how the Wave 2 inputs can be incorporated into a fast-moving, high-volume Wave 3 architecture.

Customer Experience Analytics Target Architecture

Now, let us examine the core components of the CEA target architecture. Figure 5.2 provides an overview of the reference architecture.

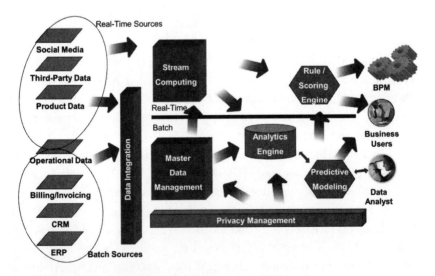

Figure 5.2: Customer experience analytics reference architecture

- *Social media*—These events are generated anywhere from public or private social media sites, such as Yelp, Facebook, and Twitter. The data is predominantly unstructured, and it provides valuable experience data as posted and shared by customers. Lately, we have seen large volumes of social media data. Stream computing and Hadoop provide tools for analyzing this data.

- *Third-party data*—This source provides business partner data. It includes location or presence information from telecommunications service providers or third-party cookie information, to name a couple of possibilities. Typically, this information is at best semi-structured and has a lot of volume to it.

- *Product data*—These events are generated from the product through customer usage and could include transaction logs from product usage, outage records, usage frequency, and so on. By and large, this information could be structured or semi-structured and is also real-time or near real-time in nature.

- *Operational data*—A number of customer-facing business processes are automated and can provide valuable information about customer interactions. In addition, supply chain information about product shipments, or products in a warehouse, in transit, purchased, and owned by a customer, can also be obtained. Some of this information changes frequently and could be structured or semi-structured.

- *Billing/Invoicing*—Information regarding customer bills, invoices, collections, receivables, and so on. This information is typically structured and comes from a billing or invoicing system.

- *Customer Relationship Management (CRM)*—Carries information about customers, products, marketing plans, campaigns, prospect data, sales contact information, customer-reported trouble, and related customer services records. This information typically comes from a packaged application and is structured data.

- *Enterprise Resource Planning (ERP)*—Carries standard information about customers, products, employees, inventory, and financial/physical assets. This information is typically structured and often comes from a standard ERP package where the data models are well-known.

- *Stream computing*—A real-time analytics system would take structured, semi-structured, or unstructured information from a variety of sources and classify, collate, or synthesize raw data to find usable information (call details, customer sentiments, events crossing a threshold, or frequent violations of product service level agreements or policies). Unlike a traditional business intelligence application, CEA systems rely on stream computing to find usable information from raw data, while the rest of the data can be either discarded or sampled for storage.

- *Master Data Management*—Provides a way to consolidate common master data from a variety of sources, each of which may cater to a particular set of users and may have different aspects of master information. Master data includes customers, products, inventory, and so on. MDM may be accompanied by tools for data synchronization, data quality management, and other related services for master data administration, search, and policy management.
- *Analytics engine*—Provides the capabilities for storing historical data as well as for executing analysis on the data. Analytics engines typically carry a staging area where the incoming information is first stored and then reorganized.
- *Rule/scoring engines*—The rule/scoring engine transforms the real-time information into a series of decisions: campaigns to be executed, advertising or coupons to be placed in front of customers, policies to be modified, or communication sent to customers. The rule base may be modified manually or automatically using predictive models.
- *Predictive models*—Predictive models provide a mechanism to study historical information and past actions to decide the most effective way to deal with customers. For example, the predictive models can infer the conditions under which customer churn may be minimized. This information is then passed on to the rule engine in the form of rules to be executed to minimize churn using policy changes or campaigns.
- *Privacy management* —Provides the policies, implementation logic, and audits for maintaining customer sensitive data. Policy management often uses data redaction, masking, or encryption to protect customer information.
- *Business Process Management (BPM)*—Provides the process for marketing, sales, operations, customer service, or trouble management. These processes are modified via rule engines.
- *Business users*—Business users include operational and senior management who would like to gain visibility into customer experience and actions taken by the CEA.

- *Data analysts*—Data analysts use the analytics engine and its query capabilities to discover ways to improve customer experience. These are the most sophisticated users of the platform and are typically the designers of the predictive models.

If we are building a brand-new greenfield infrastructure with corporate backing, it may be possible to build the entire architecture from scratch. However, those situations are rare. More than likely, an organization will go through several stages of development to get to the overall architecture. A typical development may take place in stages, which are outlined next.

Wave 1 Architecture

This architecture is depicted as a subset of the overall architecture in Figure 5.3. While the Wave 1 architecture does not provide sophisticated predictive modeling and may not be able to provide real-time access to data, it may be able to provide information that is less than one hour old, as well as powerful query capabilities to power users for initial use of the data. The Wave 1 architecture has evolved considerably using today's analytics engines. A number of appliances offer out-of-box solutions for CEA using an analytics engine, data collection, some standard reports, and ad hoc query for power users.

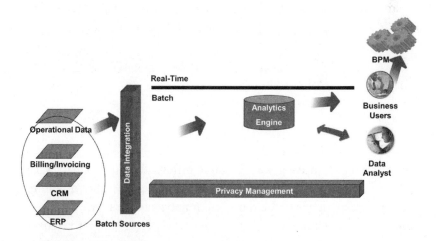

Figure 5.3: Wave 1 architecture

The typical driver for Wave 1 is a power user with a strategic informational request. The analytics engine must fulfill the use cases posed by the power users.

MDM-Driven Wave 2 Architecture

The Wave 2 architecture uses a data integration or MDM capability to harmonize across data sources. Typically customer, product, and inventory data existed within several systems. This data was synchronized and harmonized either on the MDM platform or inside the data warehouse, depending on whether the need for data synchronization is operational or informational. The resulting Wave 2 solution is capable of meeting corporate data standards and would provide capabilities to differentiate across customers. Figure 5.4 shows the Wave 2 architecture.

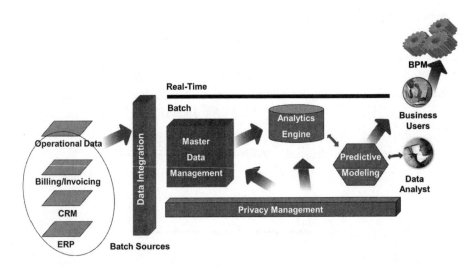

Figure 5.4: Wave 2 architecture

The typical driver for Wave 2 was customer differentiation. In Chapter 1, we discussed customer differentiation as a major mechanism for aligning good customer experience to the most important customers. Wave 2 gave us an ability to report and query the experience as perceived by the most important customers and identify specific gaps in performance that are leading to dissatisfaction or churn among these customers. The MDM function at this stage would be a separate capability in the integration layer, if there are operational users requiring common views of customer or product. However, a governance layer is needed to support the processes and organizations involved in data.

While power users can pull innovative insights from a large pool of data, predictive models provided a systematic and rigorous approach to insight development as needed for decision-making. Predictive models can start operating on the historical data stored in the analytics engine. At this stage, the decisions can be either manually entered in the business processes or carried using Predictive Model Markup Language (PMML; see Chapter 8 for details). Also, this wave included rule engines that can used to automate the execution of business logic as incorporated in the rules and modified by predictive models. For example, there may be campaigns executed by the rule engine using parameters fine-tuned by the predictive models.

Real-Time Analytics–Driven Wave 3 Architecture

The last stage in this evolution involves introduction of stream computing. So far, the processing platform was capable of collecting data and executing processes in one hour or less, which is often sufficient reaction time. However, this time duration may not be enough if we are using location-based analytics and are relying on the current location of the customer. Wave 3 provides the capabilities to speed this decision to less than a second, and in some cases to less than 10 milliseconds.

Enablers

In the next five chapters, I will detail the following enablers:

- Data movement and MDM
- Analytics engine
- Predictive modeling
- Real-time analytics
- Data privacy

These five enablers have been chosen because they provide the biggest differentiation for CEA. For each enabler, I will provide:

- *Motivation*—Why is this enabler important for CEA?
- *Enabler overview and examples*—What is the scope and role for this enabler?
- *Architectural consideration*—How will this enabler respond to the current requirements for large data and real-time?

6

Data Movement and Master Data Management

As I was discussing the virtues of CEA with an advertising executive from a telecommunications service provider, he lamented about the sorry state of source data. "I would just like to get the names, gender, age, and addresses of all my customers, and my IT organization tells me they cannot provide me with this basic information." While I agreed that he was looking for very basic demographic data, I could not help but empathize with the plight of his IT organization in bringing this information. The source systems were built for billing a customer and were extremely well established for pulling usage and account information for a paying customer. There is a big chasm to cross from account to customer and the associated demographics. My name might be the account name for a cell phone, but its user may be my daughter. She may have moved out of the house years ago to go to college. The account information is extremely accurate for the billing system, but do we have the right customer information for CEA?

Let us examine what is available within the IT department for a telecom service provider. The customer and product information is typically stored in a large number of systems; it is not uncommon to find this data in over 100 systems. I counted 11 customer IDs in one situation, each built for a specific purpose.

As Figure 6.1 shows, we have the data available in several categories of systems, each of which are represented by multiple, redundant systems representing a geographical region, an acquired company, or a business unit.

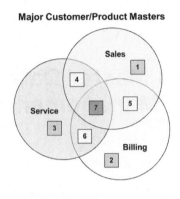

Major Customer/Product Masters

Area	Descriptions
1	Customer/Product from the point of view of Sales.
2	Customer/Product from the point of view of Billing. Includes unit rating and all pricing, taxing, and discounting rules.
3	Customer/Product from the point of view of Service, including inventory and service management. Building blocks for functional products.
4	Customer/Product information in customer products and orders, as information is conveyed from order entry to service management.
5	Customer/Product information for communication with billing system.
6	Service information conveyed to billing, including usage and third-party feeds to billing.
7	Profitability view; matching of customer, revenue, and costs to determine product and customer value.

Figure 6.1: Multiple customer and product masters

The sales systems carry account information as needed for call centers and web applications. This may include the user ID for the user managing the account, customer-facing product descriptions, and contact information. The billing systems also carry account information and sometimes deviate from sales because their focus is billing agent and billing address. The billing systems have the best understanding of the billing address, billing usage information, tax jurisdictions and discounts. The service management systems carry information on usage as well, this time more connected with inventory and resources and less with billing codes used for charging.

To obtain the best understanding of the customer, I may like to use contact information from the sales system and usage information from the service management, but can we find the right set of customer IDs to connect the two? How do we also understand customer hierarchy to decipher that we are dealing with head of household for payments and teenage children for usage information and messaging to the cell phones? Some of this information may be available from a third-party app when the teenager tries to download a cell phone ring.

Let's say, we somehow did a householding analysis and managed to use third-party information to tag all the family members. Can we still get the data for CEA? The billing system may release the data once a day at the end of a billing run, while CEA may be interested in the issues faced by this customer in the past hour (which were tracked by the network through network events) and the calls made to the call centers that resulted in customer information changes in the sales systems. In the meantime, the customer is tweeting to friends, posting information on blogs, and an entire tsunami of customer data is being generated, right from the telephone we are trying to support. We "potentially" know the location of the phone, the network it is connected to, the web sites it is connecting with. But do we really know how to digest this information, relate it to our master knowledge of the customer, and build trends to understand the customer experience?

Despite leading-edge designs for analytics engine, many programs fail due to lack of clean and current data about the environment. Lately, we are observing a data tsunami in a number of industries. Source data available from systems operated by an organization and third-party sources has increased tremendously, seriously straining organizational capabilities for ingesting and harmonization of data. In addition, much of the information needed for analytics comes from today's transactional systems, which provide a mixed bag of data with varying data quality, granularity, and frequency. In a smaller trickle of information stream, manual processes can buffer some of these issues. While these requirements are important in any analytics environment, their importance is further amplified as we increase the velocity and size of information.

The flood of information has renewed our concerns for data movement, or the lack thereof. If the data streams are flooded and require significant resolutions of customer and product IDs, chances are this data will not get cleaned up and used in time for the business processes. Wooing a customer after he or she has churned is a lot more expensive than applying corrective measures before the churn. Revenue-enhancing added products and services require time criticality, making data movement a critical path item.

Data Movement and MDM Functional Overview and Examples

The goal of Master Data Management (MDM) is to enable the vision of single, centralized or federated, master data. Through a combination of architecture, technology, and business processes, MDM provides an approach to incrementally reducing the amount of redundantly managed information and providing information consumers throughout an enterprise with authoritative master data. MDM systems that focus exclusively on managing information about customers are often called Customer Data Integration (CDI) systems. MDM systems that focus exclusively on managing the descriptions of products are called Product Information Management (PIM) systems. MDM systems that enable multiple domains of master data, and that support multiple implementation styles and methods of use, are sometimes also called Multi-Form MDM systems.[28]

The data movement may be managed by a separate Extract, Transform, and Load (ETL) application. Associated data harmonization may be achieved via a data quality tool. A change data capture application may use the change information in the source systems to synchronize the changes with the MDM system. IBM and others have started to bundle the entire set of capabilities into a single product that offers:

- *Data model for master data*—Establishing major entities and relationships needed to represent master data. Often, the tools offer a set of data modeling capabilities, leaving the specifics of the data model to the development team. Also, a number of industry models have emerged as they cover the specifics of an industry.
- *Set of services for data transformation*—The data model used by the master data may be very different from the data model used by the consuming and authoring applications. MDM products offer import and export capabilities to transform the data from source systems and into the target systems.
- *Set of services for ID and data harmonization and cleansing*—Depending on the level of diversity across source data, this may be the most important capability. Using a set of synchronization rules and logic, the software guesses whether two records relate to the

same customer or are related through a customer hierarchy. The harmonization could be based on common information, such as address, or spelling variations in the identifying information, such as first and last name. Harmonization often requires collaboration between an automated process that takes care of the majority of the cases and leaves the more ambiguous cases to a manual process.

- *Set of workflows for managing or accepting changes*—Data cleansing and MDM tools offer a set of workflows for change implementation. In the case of PIM, the changes may involve a formal process of product introduction. In the case of CDI, they may require changes to customer records that must be accepted and approved by associated account management organization.

- *Set of services for administration of the MDM*—Because these systems are used by a large number of users, both within the organization as well as outsiders, the administration systems offer capabilities for adding users, providing login credentials, and so on, including authorization levels.

- *Set of data services for search, query, and other related functions*—Data stored by the MDM can be used for search and can be used for query relating to specific customers and products. A standard set of data services offers administrators and others access to the data.

- *Audit and reporting capabilities*—MDM systems offer standard reporting capabilities as well as audit mechanisms to track changes made.

Customer Data Integration and Product Information Management combine these capabilities in somewhat different ways due to the major differences in how they manage master data. A typical CDI implementation pulls data from a variety of customer-facing systems and provides ways to harmonize the data using a common customer model. A typical PIM provides the mechanism for a set of users to collaborate in product definition and introduction process. By definition, CDI is transactional, while PIM is collaborative.

Depending on the architecture, data integration and MDM may participate in the operational systems preceding the warehouse or may be used as part of the analytics process to provide a single view of customer or product. Many analytics and reporting systems carry MDM and data integration capabilities to enhance the analytics and reporting MDM capabilities.

Figure 6.2 shows representative capabilities for a Customer Master. There are a set of operational capabilities, analytical capabilities, and supporting functions.

Figure 6.2: MDM capabilities

Operational capabilities	Analytical capabilities	Supporting functions

• Unique master entity across enterprise
• 360° customer view
• Global (enterprise-wide) customer master information/"Single Source of Truth"
• Search (fuzzy logic and parametric)
• Customer profile
• Customer relationships
• Customer leads
• Sales opportunities
• Customer contacts
• Contact history
• Service requests and complaints
• Customer maintenance
• Customer hierarchy
• Action items
• Customer life cycle management process
• Account assignment
• Hierarchy management
• Communication management
	• Customer segmentation
	• Analytical modeling
	• Customer behaviors
	• Customer communications
	• Credit analysis
	• Customer lifetime value
	• Sales tracking
	• Sales funnel management
	• Performance reports
	• Customer retention
	• Customer product profile
	• Enhance campaign effectiveness
		• Data governance and stewardship
		• Administrative functions
		  ○ Business rules management
		  ○ Security
		  ○ ID management
		  ○ User assignments
		• Data quality
		  ○ Data profiling
		  ○ De-duping
		  ○ Data parsing
		  ○ Data cleansing
		  ○ Data enrichment
		  ○ Data mgmt processes
		• Data importing and exporting
		• Compliance with governance legislation
		• SOA Compliance
		• Systems Integration (EAI/ETL)
		  ○ Sales/Marketing
		  ○ Customer service
		  ○ Billing
		  ○ Provisioning
		  ○ Business intelligence
		  ○ ERP

Key Technical Contributions

Let us start with the platform for large-scale data integration. Any environment facing massive data volumes should seriously consider the advantages of High

Performance Shared Service Grid/HA computing as a means to host their data integration infrastructures. Today, the maturity of High Performance Shared Services Grid/Stream/HA computing is such that it is now commonplace, with most companies including it in their strategic planning for architectures and enterprise data centers. The most common deployed platforms are Linux® on Intel-based grids, with AIX, Solaris, and HPUX grids following close behind. The core tenets of Grid/Stream/HA computing are the same as traditional clusters and massively parallel processing (MPP) solutions in terms of the desire to maximize the use of available hardware to complete a processing task. However, what is new about the IBM Information Server Grid/HA and InfoSphere Streams environments is their ease of setup and use, the unlimited linear scalability to thousands of nodes, the fully dynamic load node/pod balancing/execution, the ability to achieve automatic high availability/disaster recovery (HA/DR), and the much lower price points at which you can achieve comparable performance of traditional symmetric multiprocessing (SMP) shared memory server configurations. The overall adoption of grid computing is now becoming commonplace, and it is accelerating, driven by the price-to-performance statistics, flexibility, and economics. The key to the success of Grid/Stream/HA Shared Service implementations lies in the entire solution working for the business providing straight through processing (STP) with dynamic process allocation, flexibility, and scale-up. A typical parallel data integration platform:

- Designs integration process without concern for data volumes or time constraints
- Leverages database partitioning schemes for optimal load performance
- Simplifies steps to define partitions within each process if needed
- Uses a single configuration file to add processors and hardware
- Requires no hand coding of programs to enable more processors
- Supports SMP, clustered, Grid, and MPP platforms

Figure 6.3 depicts the parallel data integration platform.

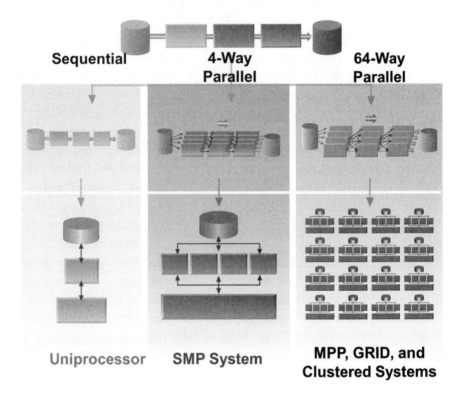

Figure 6.3: Parallel data integration platform

Now, let us move toward Master Data Management. Gartner had categorized four styles of MDM implementation: registry, coexistence, centralized, and consolidation.[29] Gartner and others have debated and studied different implementation styles and the conditions under which one style is preferred over another. As we increase the velocity and volume of heterogeneous data, it directly impacts the activities MDM can undertake in the time allotted to the MDM. The best implementation style for this environment is the registry style, described by John Ratcliff as follows:

- Low control, autonomous environments
- Nonintrusive of edge applications

- Emphasis on remote data and application-to-application integration (lots of real-time network access)
- Distributed governance
- Faster to implement than coexistence and centralized[30]

The healthcare industry is a classic example of a distributed information environment where the registry style MDM is the best approach. In Chapter 1, we covered the University of Pittsburgh Medical Center's EMPI data. For regional and national information banks, the household information and patient relationships would be very useful. What we need is a strong harmonization capability that can be used to align patient records to a household and be saved for a variety of analysis.

Let me use Initiate as an example to show harmonization capabilities available in the MDM products. While other MDM products were attempting centralized customer masters, Initiate evolved in a distributed environment where the basic purpose of the MDM was to take customer data from diverse organizations and assemble a single set of IDs to connect these diverse records together. A classic example is the healthcare industry, where the patient data comes from a variety of sources—hospitals, doctor's offices, and pharmacies, to name a few—and needs to be assimilated by the healthcare insurer for claims processing. Initiate provides capabilities for matching these customer records using the field information. The matched records can be combined into a master record with links to the matched records from the source system.

The heart of the offering is Initiate Inspector™[31]. This application enables data stewards and data managers to view, manage, and create relationships between different data types. It is tightly integrated with data resolution so data stewards can be certain that the relationships they are managing are based on a single, trusted view of the data. This integration further benefits data stewards through visual alerts that records involved in relationships may have data quality issues—data stewards can navigate between relationship and data resolution to ensure they are making business decisions using the best data possible. Data stewardship involves many concepts and functions, including:

- Reviewing records to ensure the data is accurate, and correcting or updating the data if necessary
- Resolving data integrity issues, including duplicate records and potential record overlays (overwrite existing record with a new record)
- Ensuring the quality of records coming from source systems by searching for the source records, reviewing their data, and entering missing data
- Reviewing link decisions to verify that auto-link thresholds are configured and performing as expected in the policies
- Making manual linkage decisions when necessary

Inspector has three main purposes:

- *Resolving tasks:*
  o It enables data stewards to understand data quality issues and resolve tasks.
  o It can resolve tasks using a simple, drag-and-drop interface. If you are upgrading from Initiate Auditor, Inspector has the same functionality in a simpler user interface that is easier to use and requires fewer clicks to resolve each task.
- *Managing relationships:*
  o It enables data stewards to view, manage, and modify complex master data relationships, including hierarchical relationships.
- *Managing data:*
  o Add completely new records from scratch (e.g., implementation testing phases)
  o Modify existing records; view different sets of values, fill in missing values, correct simple typographical errors, and so on

Harmonization will be an essential ingredient to Customer Experience Analytics as more and more sources for data turn inter-organizational. For example, consider the patient records that we discussed in the healthcare scenarios in Chapter 1. The health insurance may have an elaborate relationship model of the household, with all the relationships across family members and their insurance coverage. This data may also be used to understand diseases across family members. Children may inherit genetic diseases from their parents, and people living in the same house may be susceptible to catching contagious diseases from each other. Each of these family members may be a patient of a number of service providers, each of whom may have a link to the insurance ID but could have different name spellings and other variations in their records. As the insurance company assimilates and assembles the information, the family hierarchy may provide clues about how to align the records and fix anomalies in the records imported from other providers (see Figure 6.4).

| Source 1 | Bob Smith | 123 Main Street | Son |
| Source 2 | Robert Smith | 123 Main Street | Patient |

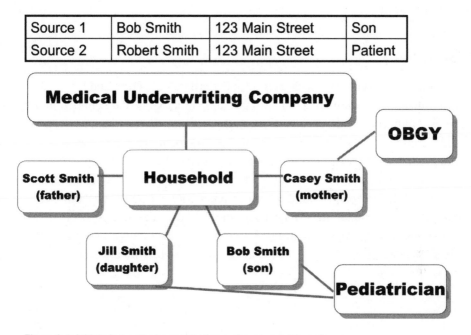

Figure 6.4: Initiate Inspector harmonization and customer hierarchy

Initiate Inspector provides sophisticated algorithms for harmonization. A simple example would be Bob Smith and Robert Smith as variations to the same name. Each set of harmonized records receives a probability of match, and, depending on the policy, the results of the match are automatically accepted, automatically rejected, or sent to a steward for further analysis. The resulting harmonized records are passed on to the target environment for analytics. The required level of accuracy changes from industry to industry and from one application to another. If the only purpose of the harmonization is to store raw data for statistical analysis, 1 percent error may by acceptable in certain situations. If the purpose of the harmonization is to decide on medical treatment or make a payment, a small error may not be acceptable.

In a number of situations, the names and addresses are not as important as the structure of the relationships—whether we deal with households, subsidiaries of a company, or a social network. Each source carries data associated with individuals in a network. MDM is the powerful glue that organizes and categorizes this data into a set of meaningful relationships for further analysis or correlations.

Summary

This chapter provided us with useful tools for data collection and harmonization. With increasing volumes and velocity, the data collection may involve hundreds or thousands of parallel processors that collect, reorganize, and cleanse the data and deliver it to the downstream analytics engines and predictive models. Data integration and MDM tools offer important capabilities for transforming and harmonizing source data and often cleanse the data. A CDI capability organizes customer data, while PIM establishes common product data. MDM systems offer data services and export this data to various consuming applications. Using parallel data integration platforms, the associated products have scaled to current-day volumes and velocity of the data.

CHAPTER 7

Stream Computing

Traditional computing was built on a batch paradigm. Consider, for example, a call center. All the customer call information was collected at the call center and extracted, transformed, and loaded into a data warehouse, which provided trend analysis and reporting on the call center data. How many customers called in a particular day? What was the average wait time? What was the average handling time? Did the customer provide feedback at the end of the call? How many rated us a 1, or "very poor"? Was that trend up or down from prior days?

Increasingly, however, call centers are moving to an event-driven, continuous intelligence view of operations. This approach enables immediate detection and correction of problems as they appear, rather than after-the-fact changes.

For example, an agent dealing with a customer who has been transferred several times or has been on hold for more than five minutes can be prompted (and allowed) to give additional compensation for the negative experience. The contact center software may also generate "screen popups" to prompt agents to ask customer-specific questions to drive up-selling or cross-selling. If feedback indicates that an agent was irate, a supervisor may be alerted to give the agent an early break to recover.[32]

Stream computing is a new paradigm. In "traditional" processing, one can think of running analytic queries against historical data—for instance, calculate the distance walked last month from a data set of subscribers who transmit GPS location data while walking. With stream computing, one can execute a process similar to a "continuous query" that keeps running totals, as location information from GPS data is refreshed moment by moment. In the first case, questions are asked of historical data, while in the second case data is continuously evaluated via static questions (see Figure 7.1).

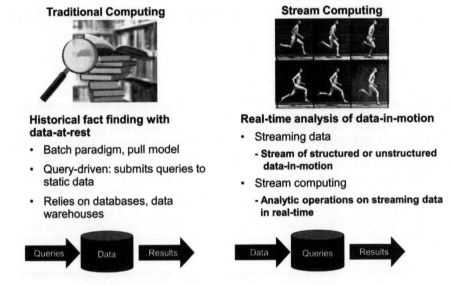

Traditional Computing

Historical fact finding with data-at-rest

- Batch paradigm, pull model
- Query-driven: submits queries to static data
- Relies on databases, data warehouses

Stream Computing

Real-time analysis of data-in-motion

- Streaming data
  - Stream of structured or unstructured data-in-motion
- Stream computing
  - Analytic operations on streaming data in real-time

Figure 7.1: Traditional computing vs. stream computing

Stream Computing Functional Overview and Examples

Why is there a sudden interest in stream computing? After a number of years of research work, we have started to identify a large number of real-world problems where the traditional data warehouse platform fails to scale to the volume of data and velocity of decision-making. The need for stream computing is pervasive. Figure 7.2 shows a number of applications across industries, including natural systems, stock market, law enforcement, fraud prevention, radio astronomy, telecom, health and life sciences, manufacturing, and transportation.

The Need for New Intelligence Is Everywhere...

Natural Systems
• Seismic monitoring
• Wildfire management
• Water management

Stock Market
• Impact of weather on securities prices
• Analyze market data at ultra-low latencies

Law Enforcement
• Real-time multimodal surveillance

Transportation
• Intelligent traffic management

Fraud Prevention
• Detecting multi-party fraud
• Real-time fraud prevention

Manufacturing
• Process control for microchip fabrication

Radio Astronomy
• Detection of transient events

Health & Life Science
• Neonatal ICU monitoring
• Epidemic early warning system
• Remote healthcare monitoring

Telecom
• Processing of call detail records
• Real-time services, billing, advertising
• Business intelligence
• Churn analysis, fraud detection

Figure 7.2: Sample stream computing applications

These applications show three common characteristics:

- *High volume of data*—Faster than a database can handle
- *Complex analytics*—Correlation from multiple sources and/or signals (video, audio, or other non-relational data types)
- *Time-sensitive*—Responses required with low latency

Customer experience is an ideal area for applying stream computing. The number of events created by the customer or the environment is staggering. We are seeking patterns associated with a customer by analyzing a chain of events as they occur. Stream computing not only allows us to analyze and identify the context of a customer behavior; it also provides certain actions that up-sell, cross-sell, encourage, or prohibit customer actions based on pre-specified criteria. These criteria can be changed over time because stream computing can adapt to changes in the environment. For example, if a customer is driving on a highway that is experiencing traffic due to weather conditions, stream computing can be used to sense the traffic pattern changes and offer alternative routes. A traffic management system may use a number of real-time data feeds (see Figure 7.3):

- GPS
- Cell phones (location tracking)
- Public transport (bus, docking)
- Pollution measurements
- Weather conditions (including road conditions)
- Optical traffic flow detectors
- Travel time data based on plate recognition
- Induction loop detector data
- Accidents in the network as they are being recorded
- Road closures (e.g., roadwork)
- Still pictures from road cameras

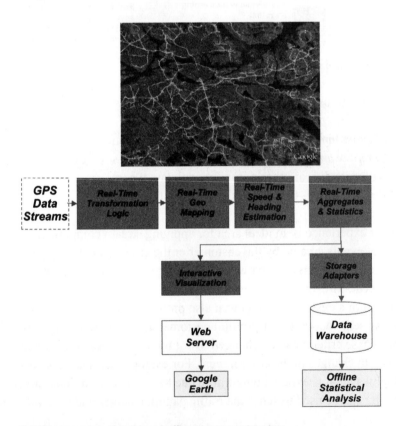

Figure 7.3: Stream computing driven traffic management system

Let us examine stream computing using the architectural constructs of InfoSphere Streams:

- A programming model for defining data flow graphs consisting of *data sources* (inputs), *operators*, and *sinks* (outputs)
- Controls for fusing operators into *processing elements* (PEs)
- Infrastructure to support the composition of scalable *stream processing applications* from these components
- Deployment and operation of these applications across distributed *x86 processing nodes*, when scaled-up processing is required

In InfoSphere Streams, continuous applications are composed of individual operators, which interconnect and operate on one or more data streams. Data streams normally come from outside the system or can be produced internally as part of an application. Figure 7.4 shows chains of operators that work on input streams of data and fuse into PEs. The operators may be used on the data to have it filtered, classified, transformed, correlated, and/or fused to make decisions using business rules.

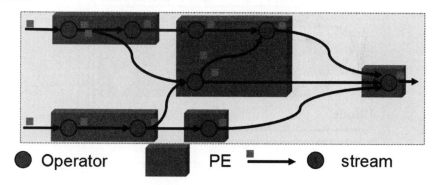

Figure 7.4: Operators, streams, and processing elements

These operators are developed in Streams Processing Language (SPL) using a development environment and compiled into a run-time code. At run-time, InfoSphere Streams uses the following constructs to execute (see Figure 7.5):

- *Instance*
  - o Runtime instantiation of InfoSphere Streams executing across one or more hosts
  - o Collection of components and services
- *PE*
  - o Fundamental execution unit that is run by the Streams instance
  - o Can encapsulate a single operator or many "fused" operators
- *Job*
  - o A deployed Streams application executing in an instance
  - o Consists of one or more PEs

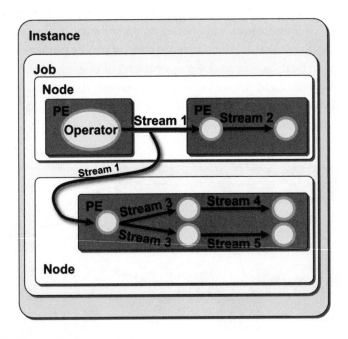

Figure 7.5: Stream objects – run-time view

Key Technical Contributions

Every day, we create 2.5 quintillion bytes of data—so much that 90 percent of the data in the world today has been created in the past two years alone. This data comes from everywhere: sensors used to gather climate information, posts on social media sites, digital pictures and videos posted online, transaction records of online purchases, and cell phone GPS signals, to name a few.[33] The New York Stock Exchange generates about 1 terabyte of new trade data per day. Facebook hosts approximately 10 billion photos, taking up 1 petabyte of storage. Ancestry.com, a genealogy site, stores around 2.5 petabytes of data. The Internet Archive stores around 2 petabytes of data and is growing at a rate of 20 terabytes per month. The Large Hadron Collider near Geneva, Switzerland, will produce about 15 petabytes of data per year. There is a lot of data out there.[34]

Big data spans three dimensions: variety, velocity, and volume.

- *Variety*—Big data extends beyond structured data to include unstructured data of all varieties: text, audio, video, click streams, log files, and more.
- *Velocity*—Often time-sensitive, big data must be used as it is streaming into the enterprise in order to maximize its value to the business.
- *Volume*—Big data comes in one size: large. Enterprises are awash with data, easily amassing terabytes and even petabytes of information.

Stream computing excels in each of these dimensions. It works with a variety of data structures: structured or unstructured text, audio, and video information. It achieves volume through parallel processing. In the case of InfoSphere Streams, the software runs on commodity hardware—from single nodes to blade centers to high-performance multi-rack clusters. Blades can be added or subtracted from the run-time environment based on workload. Each operator may run on one or more blades using Processing Element Containers that are distributed across the blades. An optimizing scheduler assigns operators to processing nodes and continually manages resource allocation.

Stream computing requires a very lean programming environment to achieve velocity. For example, InfoSphere Streams uses compiled C++ and can execute using in-memory data structures in microseconds. Thus, a large-scale task involving matching of in-memory structures to an incoming stream of data, or scoring a number of models using pre-established scoring models, can be done in real-time.

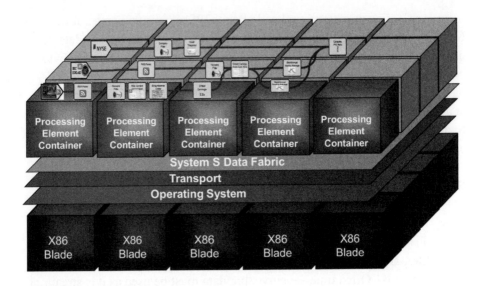

Figure 7.6: Run-time services for parallel processing

CHAPTER 8

Predictive Modeling

Predictive modeling provides the capability to analyze historical data to predict future behavior. Advances in statistics, psychology, and the science of social networks are giving researchers the tools to find patterns of human dynamics too subtle to detect by other means.

At Northeastern University in Boston, network physicists discovered just how predictable people could be by studying the travel routines of 100,000 European mobile-phone users. After analyzing more than 16 million records of call date, time, and location, the researchers determined that, taken together, people's movements appeared to follow a mathematical pattern. The researchers said that, with enough information about past movements, they could forecast someone's future whereabouts with 93.6 percent accuracy.[35]

This type of analytics radically differs from the classic reports-driven information creation. It is within our ability to find a set of decision trees in the past customer experience data and use them to offer further-refined customer experience. Predictive modeling has the following advantages:

- It makes predictions, such as who is likely to churn and what can be done in actions to prevent the churn.
- The impact is conveyed via "point of impact"—typically a customer touch point—by making policy changes, executing a process, or communicating with the customer (e.g., by offering personalized coupons on the cell phone at the grocery store).

- The results are executed by everyone, whether it is a call-center service representative offering the "next best action" or a web site customizing web pages to the specific need of a customer.
- The actions are performed in real-time. I get a call from my telecommunications service provider if the bandwidth of my Internet connection is slow, before I have a chance to call the competition and switch my service.
- The actions are optimized. We provide the best service to our most profitable/loyal customers.

True predictive capability is absent, or at best rudimentary, in traditional industry solutions. As a result, organizations focus on sensing and then responding to issues, which is a reactive stance. Often, the damage (churn, fraudulent activity, excessive marketing spend) has already occurred, and the goal then becomes to minimize the impact on the organization. Traditional organizations also often rely on the instinct and intuition of resident experts rather than using objective evidence that is grounded in data to guide decision-making, despite empirical evidence showing that statistical models consistently out-predict the experts. Many analytical systems also often require specialized skills or training, limiting their use to a select number of individuals within an organization and constraining the analytic activity to back-office functions rather than positioning it at the critical point of impact. Automation is also widely touted in traditional systems. Although the ability to automate is important, even more important is the optimization of decisions, or making the right decision at the right moment (Figure 8.1).[36]

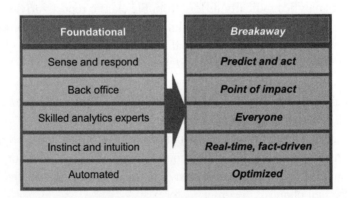

Figure 8.1: Paradigm shift powered by predictive modeling

Predictive Modeling Functional Overview and Examples

Predictive modeling contributes to these decisions using three distinct stages (depicted in Figure 8.2):

1. *Capture*—Collects data about customer behaviors
2. *Predict*—Uses a set of techniques such as text mining, data mining, statistics, etc., to seek patterns.
3. *Act*—Uses a wide variety of deployment technologies to respond to customer behavior in real-time with actions that provide optimal product or service experience.

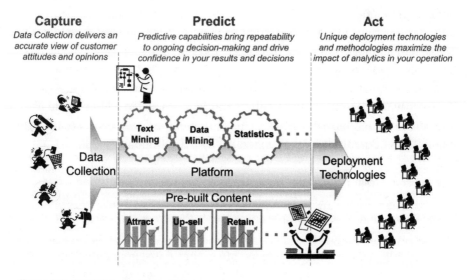

Figure 8.2: Predictive modeling stages

A classic predictive modeling example was described by Gordon Linoff.[37] Bank of America's (BoA's) home equity lines of credit were failing to attract enough good customers. There were several ways the bank could attack this problem. The National Consumer Assets Group (NCAG) decided to use data mining to attack the problem, providing a good introduction to the virtuous cycle of data mining. BoA needed to do a better job of marketing home equity loans to customers. Using common sense and business consultants, it came up with these insights:

- People with college-aged children want to borrow against their home equity to pay tuition bills.
- People with high but variable incomes want to use home equity to smooth out the peaks and valleys in their income.

For many years, BoA had been storing data on millions of its retail customers. Data from 42 systems of records was cleansed, transformed, aligned, and fed into the corporate data warehouse. With this system, BoA could see all the relationships each customer maintained with the bank. Recent customer records had about 250 fields, including demographic fields such as income, number of children, and type of home, as well as internal data. Decision trees derived rules to classify existing bank customers as likely or unlikely to respond to a home equity loan offer. The decision tree, trained on thousands of examples of customers who had obtained the product and thousands who had not, eventually learned rules to tell the difference between them. After the rules were discovered, the resulting model was used to add yet another attribute to each prospect's record. This attribute, the "good prospect for home equity lines of credit flag," was generated by a data mining model.

Next, a sequential pattern-finding technique was used to determine when customers were most likely to want a loan of this type. The goal of this analysis was to discover a sequence of events that frequently preceded successful solicitations in the past. Finally, a clustering technique was used to automatically segment the customers into groups with similar attributes. At one point, the tool found 14 clusters of customers, many of which did not seem particularly interesting. Of these 14 clusters, though, one had two intriguing properties:

- 39 percent of the people in the cluster had both business and personal accounts.
- This cluster accounted for more than a quarter of the customers who had been classified by the decision tree as likely responders to a home equity loan offer.

These results suggested to inquisitive data miners that people might be using home equity loans to start businesses. As a result, NCAG changed the message of its campaign from "Use the value of your home to send your kids to college" to something more along the lines of "Now that the house is empty, use your equity to do what you've always wanted to do." With the improved focus of the marketing campaign, the response rate for home equity campaigns increased from 0.7 percent to 7 percent.

Cablecom is a large Swiss cable network operator with 1.6 million customers. Over 54 percent of Swiss television households receive cable service from Cablecom. The company faced a highly competitive marketplace and a high churn rate. As Cablecom studied its churn rate, it discovered:

- It had high cancellation rate at the end of the initial contract.
- It could reduce churn by identifying the point at which customers become dissatisfied with the service and before they made the decision to switch to an alternative provider.
- This analytics would help Cablecom better understand customers and anticipate market trends.

Cablecom used IBM's SPSS Modeler, SPSS Survey application, and Text Analytics to analyze customer feedback. It incorporated this analytics into its enterprise feedback program and used predictive analytics technology to better understand customers in terms of characteristics, behaviors, and attitudes. The company analyzed customer feedback across various phases of the customer lifecycle. It now uses this insight to predict future behavior and adapt its customer-facing activities to meet customer demands and cut churn.

As a result, Cablecom saw a churn reduction from 19 percent to 2 percent for its broadband subscribers. Its churn model was able to predict customers likely to churn with a 78 percent accuracy. Satisfaction increased among more than 50 percent of Cablecom customers, and 23 percent of "detractors" converted to "promoters."

Here are some details on the model used by Cablecom. The company conducted a survey with a sample of customers, asking each of them how satisfied they were with Cablecom services. Customers who provided "poor" scores were asked to state factors that resulted in the poor scores. The customers who provided "good" scores were asked to provide factors that resulted in the good scores. The survey information was combined with customer information, including network performance, bills, demographics, and other data. The team used a predictive model to analyze reasons for churn and made recommendations based on the model. The model is detailed below (also see Figure 8.3):

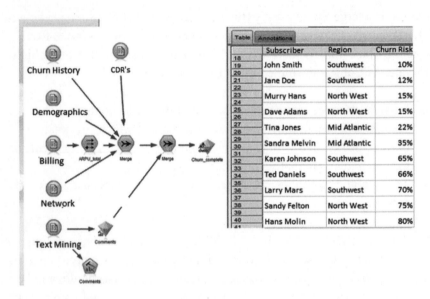

Figure 8.3: Predictive modeling – CEA example

- *Capture*—A holistic view of the customer, including:
  - *Churn history*—Historical information on churn. Which customers are defecting and why?
  - *CDRs*—Call detail records.
  - *Demographics*—Information about customer's geography, income, age, family size, and so on.
  - *Billing data*—Information about customer product purchases and use.
  - *Network*—Any associated data from the telecommunications network supporting the customer. Through network information, we can infer quality of service.

- o *Text mining*—Data from customer surveys is scanned and mined for key words.
- **Predict**—At this stage, the input data is used for analysis and scoring:
  - o *Analysis*—The survey customers are divided.
  - o *Scoring*—The customer data are then matched with a variety of offers, and the predictive model estimated the likelihood of churn reduction based on historical success of the offer on similar profiled customers.
- **Act**—Acting on the results of analysis. This involves the following actions:
  - o *Drive campaigns and interactions*—Combining the results of possibly multiple models with business logic (e.g., rules, policies, exclusions) to arbitrate between different possible actions and decide on the right campaign to be used for a customer or "next best action" in the customer contact center.[38]

Predictive Modeling: Selective Deep Dive

By design, predictive modeling is a deeper (read "slower") process that works with enormous amounts of historical data. For example, consider the statistician on the staff of a sports show who makes the commentator's job more colorful. As games and sports are occurring, the commentator describes the events, while the statistician works in the background to update statistics and looks for relevant trends and changes. As anything of significance becomes available, it is made known to the commentator, who then uses the statistics in the course of the normal commentary.

CEA must work in pretty much the same way. The predictive modeling engine works in the background using the data accumulating in the analytics engine. As the data results in significant predictive changes or new trends to be used for the scoring of events, these inferences are passed on to the stream computing or the rule engine.

So, how do we enable the statistician to work with the real-time components? Data Mining Group (DMG), a vendor-led consortium with full membership from IBM, SAS, and Microstrategy, has created PMML, a standard for data mining modeling. PMML provides applications with a vendor-independent method of defining models so that proprietary issues and incompatibilities are no longer a barrier to the exchange of models between applications. It allows users to develop models within one vendor's application and use other vendors' applications to visualize, analyze, evaluate, or otherwise use the models. Previously, this was very difficult, but with PMML, the exchange of models between compliant applications is now straightforward.[39] Here are some of the testimonials posted on the DMG web site, expressing how PMML supports the task of incorporating predictive models into corresponding real-time components:

"PMML turns the deployment and practical application of predictive models within any existing IT infrastructure into reality, unleashing the power of those models. Without PMML, it would take months for models to be integrated and deployed via custom code or proprietary processes and at very high additional cost."
—*Cris Payne, Senior Analytics Scientist for XO Communications, Inc.*

"PMML frees model deployment from the shackles of model development. As a well-established open standard for model representation, PMML is enabling a new generation of data mining deployment environments in business intelligence products, data warehouses, and cloud computing."
—*Graham Williams, Togaware Pty, Ltd.*

The current version (4.0) of PMML supports a number of statistical models:

- Association Model
- General Regression Model
- Mining Model
- Naïve Bayes Model
- Neural Network
- Regression Model
- Ruleset Model

- Sequence Model
- Support Vector Machine Model
- Text Model
- Time Series Model
- Tree Model

As long as the predictive modeling tool and the corresponding real-time component support the current version of PMML, the models can be discovered by the predictive model and promoted to be used by the real-time component. Thus, as in the sports show analogy, the statistician can work in the back room and add new predictive models.

The promotion process can be supported by a rigorous experiment design. The practitioners have been using the Champion-Challenger model for a long time in their manual promotion process. In a typical Champion-Challenger model, a set of models currently used in the production environment are labeled "Champion." These are the current, approved, accepted models for customer experience modeling. At the same time, the statisticians run an experiment design using a set of newly discovered models labeled "Challengers." The experiment design is typically done using a sample small enough not to make a dent in the production environment, but large enough to be statistically significant. Let us say we randomly choose 200 households out of 10 million and use the "Challenger" model for these experimental households. If the performance of the Challenger is significantly better than the Champion, the Challenger replaces the Champion for the entire population and the process is repeated.

Predictive modeling tools have used PMML to automate the Champion-Challenger promotion process, whereby the task of comparison, analysis, and promotion of the Challenger can be performed automatically. It allows us to have better governance of the predictive models and how they are introduced or removed in the production environment.

9

Analytics Engines and Appliances

As analytics evolved, the platforms included a number of hardware, software, and storage components. Consultants and IT organizations started to mix and match these components for the optimal mix to create a data warehouse platform that best matched the performance and cost criteria. However, this mixing-and-matching process generated large program costs and often failed to produce the right results. A number of analytics engine/appliances have emerged in the past decade. These appliances can be defined by four characteristics:

- They have only one purpose.
- They are contained within one package.
- They require one installation of their technology.
- There is only one vendor to call for maintenance and support.[40]

These analytics engines pre-package hardware, software, and storage components and sometimes even bundle it all on the Cloud. For example, the Netezza analytics appliance offered by IBM combines hardware, software, and storage in a pre-packaged way for different sizes of storage. The analytics engines have radically reduced time to develop initial pilot systems while providing unstructured, out-of-box query capabilities. Figure 9.1 shows a comparison of the Netezza Analytics engine with custom combination of software and hardware. While the analytics engines streamline the development and implementation process, they lack the flexibility offered by traditional data warehouse platforms.

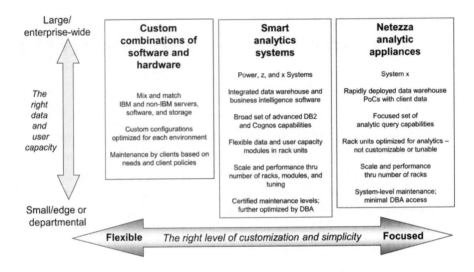

Figure 9.1: Spectrum of analytics engines

Analytics Engine: Functional Overview and Examples

Why would we trade the flexibility of a mix-and-match data warehouse platform for an analytics engine? The next series of examples will demonstrate the benefits of an analytics engine.

MediaMath has developed an automated buying platform to provide advertising agencies with access to more than 13 billion impressions daily and a simple workflow that manages the powerful analytics and rich data necessary to make best use of them. Headquartered in New York, the company was founded in 2007 by a team of seasoned entrepreneurs, marketers, technologists, and quants. The Netezza TwinFin® appliance's simple workflow and ability to scale to more than a petabyte of data makes it the ideal solution for MediaMath, which has integrated five real-time bidding sources (the most in the industry), over a dozen third-party data and dynamic creative partners, and an advanced optimization platform that calculates the fair market value of over 50,000 impressions per second.[41]

Catalina Marketing maintains the largest loyalty database in the world, with more than 600 billion rows of data in a single table; its data warehousing environment shot past the petabyte mark seven years ago and today stands at 2.5 PB. Catalina's single largest database contains three years' worth of purchase history for 195 million U.S. customer-loyalty-program members at supermarkets, pharmacies, and other retailers. At the cash registers of Catalina's retail customers, real-time analysis of that data triggers printouts of coupons that shoppers are handed with their receipt at checkout. Each coupon is unique; two shoppers checking out one after the other, with identical items in their carts, will get different coupons based on their buying histories in combination with third-party demographic data.

There is a theme in that example: customers drive vendors into partnerships. Three years ago, Catalina was among the customers that led to Netezza and SAS working together on in-database processing. Statisticians typically sample 10 percent to 15 percent of a customer base to build a model. With a loyalty database of 195 million consumers, Catalina in some cases needed hundreds of terabytes just to build a model—more data than most companies have in their entire data warehouse. The two vendors collaborated on a Scoring Accelerator for Netezza, which they introduced early this year and which Catalina adopted. "Before, we were lucky if we could develop 50 to 60 models per year," says Eric Williams, CIO and executive VP at Catalina. "Because of the in-database technology, we believe we'll be able to do 600 models per year with the same staff."[42]

Each and every day, T-Mobile processes 17 billion events, including phone calls, text messages, and data. That high-impact, high-profile data crunching recently won the operator an award at IBM's Netezza Enzee Universe event. The number is impressive, and according to Anthony Behan, global analytics solution owner at IBM worldwide, "Last year the figure was 11 billion, so we have seen an increase of 6 billion transactions per day over the last year. Next year, who knows exactly what the figure will be." Those 17 billion transactions are sent to a 1.2 petabyte database, crunched using the Netezza application, and then presented to various T-Mobile internal users.

This represents one of the first examples of telcos doing what telcos should do best: taking the data that they already process in a simple way and transforming that data into information that can be used to increase the efficiency of the business using CEA. At the moment, T-Mobile is using this information to make better use of its network assets, making sure that the quality and capacity is where it is needed. CDR and broadband probes are monitored, and the data is cross-referenced across the enterprise. Significant amounts of money are being saved along the way.

Optimizing the network was the first phase in this project, but it is interesting that once this huge amount of data was in the right place at the right time in the right way, it went viral. The information is being accessed and used by more and more executives across the business. Currently numbering around 1,200, the users include people from finance and corporate accounts as well as sales and marketing. This is just the beginning. Understanding and optimizing the network is one important application. T-Mobile plans to use this information and other data to start the journey toward true personalization. Understanding customers completely and individually will ultimately enable T-Mobile and others to maximize the value of services and to place the right value on those services, thus optimizing revenues.[43]

Analytics Engine: Selective Deep Dive

These applications require a fair amount of storage capacity and raw unstructured query capabilities. The Netezza Analytics Engine schematic, as shown in Figure 9.2, shines in large-scale analytics applications. Data warehouse appliances architecturally integrate database, server, and storage components into a single unit.

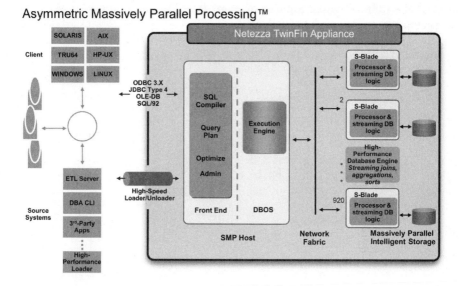

Figure 9.2: Netezza architecture

The Netezza Performance Server (NPS®) system's architecture is a two-tiered system designed to handle very large queries from multiple users. The first tier is a high-performance Linux symmetric multiprocessing host. The host compiles queries received from business intelligence applications and generates query execution plans. It then divides a query into a sequence of subtasks, or snippets, which can be executed in parallel, and it distributes the snippets to the second tier for execution. The host returns the final results to the requesting application, thus providing the programming advantages while appearing to be a traditional database server.

The second tier consists of dozens to hundreds or thousands of Snippet Processing Units (SPUs) operating in parallel. Each SPU is an intelligent query processing and storage node and consists of a powerful commodity processor, dedicated memory, a disk drive, and a field-programmable disk controller with hard-wired logic to manage data flows and process queries at the disk level, as depicted in Figure 9.3.

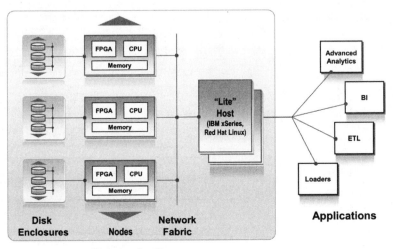

Figure 9.3: The Netezza AMPP™ Architecture

The massively parallel, shared-nothing SPU blades provide the performance advantages of massively parallel processors. Nearly all query processing is done at the SPU level, with each SPU operating on its portion of the database. All operations that easily lend themselves to parallel processing (including record operations, parsing, filtering, projecting, interlocking, and logging) are performed by the SPU nodes, which significantly reduces the amount of data moved within the system. Operations on sets of intermediate results, such as sorts, joins, and aggregates, are executed primarily on the SPUs but can also be done on the host, depending on the processing cost of that operation.

Intelligent Query Streaming™ is performed on each SPU by a Field-Programmable Gate Array (FPGA) chip that functions as the disk controller, but which is also capable of basic processing as data is read from the disk. The system is able to run critical database query functions such as parsing, filtering, and projecting at full disk reading speed while maintaining full Atomicity, Consistency, Isolation, and Durability (ACID) transactional operations of the database. Data flows from disk to memory in a single laminar stream, rather than as a series of disjointed steps that would require materializing partial results.

To achieve high performance, the storage interconnection, which is a bottleneck with traditional systems, is eliminated by directly attaching the disks so that data can stream straight into the FPGA for initial query filtering. Then, to further reduce the workload on the central server, the intermediate query tasks are performed in parallel on the SPUs. The internal network traffic has been reduced by approximately two orders of magnitude by using the system-wide, gigabit Ethernet network to transmit only intermediate results, rather than the entire collection of raw data. As a result, the input/output (I/O) bus and memory bus on the host computer are used only to assemble final results.

In general-purpose systems, I/O bottlenecks are commonplace as the system is scaled to accommodate complex queries. On the other hand, in this architecture, additional arrays of SPUs can be added to the NPS system without impacting I/O performance because query processing involves just a minute fraction of the data traffic associated with traditional systems, and because storage and processing are tightly coupled into a single unit. The autonomy of the SPUs creates further conditions for a highly scalable system, allowing SPUs to be added without worrying about coordination with other units. As a result, growing data volumes can be managed and accommodated with orderly, predictable investments.

Davidson et al. report an evaluation of the Netezza Performance Server 8150 with 108 active SPUs, each with its own disk, which holds 1/108th of the database. By uniformly distributing the data across all of the disks, the applications can make use up to 4.5 terabytes for one large database or an aggregate combination of different databases.[44]

Summary

The advantages to Netezza appliance users are as follows:

- The ad hoc query processing is blazingly faster on the Netezza appliance. In field tests, Netezza has repeatedly shown 10X to 100X processing speed compared with a typical data warehouse.
- The maintenance cost is much less on the Netezza appliance. Because the appliance does not require constant fine-tuning of database indices, the warehouse can be maintained with a significantly smaller number of DBAs.
- It can deal with semi-structured data. As data warehouses move from internally focused (CRM, ERP, billing) to externally focused (social media, third parties), the data structures are at best semi-structured. The relaxation in data modeling allows Netezza users to fully use its potential for externally focused data.
- In many cases, the users are a combination of power users performing ad hoc queries and predictive modeling tools mining the data. The out-of-box ad hoc query capabilities are the first love for power users. Also, predictive modeling tools are increasingly using the data warehouse's SQL capabilities to do most of the model crunching in the data warehouse instead of extracting it into a separate data mining environment. Appliances are beginning to offer this capability. The Netezza appliance offers scalability through in-database execution. Applications that can take advantage of this capability, such as the SPSS Modeler Premium, Cognos® push-down, and bespoke customer applications, should build on the Netezza appliance for this capability.
- If an IT organization is new to data architecture, they will appreciate the simplicity and appliance nature of Netezza. Without building large IT organizations, they can build an analytics solution.
- The scale model for the Netezza appliance is a straightforward factor based on the number of S-Blades in the system and the volume of data that must be processed to compute the query response. A query on a TwinFin 12 with 12 S-Blades will run twice as fast on a TwinFin 24 with two times the number of S-Blades. As data volumes grow over time, analytic query response times are very predictable on the Netezza TwinFin appliance.

- Predictable analytic query response times on the Netezza appliance allow managed service providers and IT organizations to meet service level agreements for analytic query processing.
- The Netezza appliance allows new tables to be loaded and immediately queried against or joined with existing data sets or tables. There are no indexes in the Netezza appliance that have to be defined or generated. This also allows any table to be joined with any other table at any time.

CHAPTER **10**

Privacy Management

Privacy is the biggest spoiler in the CEA world. Given the amount of data we are collecting, the amount of modeling we are doing, and the impact we can have on the customer, a privacy waiver in the fine print is the worst way of providing the customer with a big shock. On the other hand, customers are very willing to opt-in if it makes them richer, happier, or smarter without inappropriate use of the data by third parties. There are different ways in which vertical markets are dealing with privacy today, and there are significant geopolitical differences.

Before we examine the architecture for managing CEA privacy, let us first look at the factors driving customer privacy concerns in more detail:

- *Regulations*—As we discussed in Chapter 2, other than the debt ceiling, location privacy is the hottest regulatory debate item in the United States in 2011. There are a significant number of regulations at the U.S. federal and state level covering how customer data should be stored and exposed, and what to do in case of data breach.
- *Cost of data breach*—If, despite all precautions, customer data is inadvertently leaked or stolen, specific regulatory guidelines apply regarding communication to the customer. The situation may also result in bad customer perception and could result in customer churn. A reactive fix to customer privacy is an order of magnitude more expensive than a proactive policy and execution.

- *Sharing of customer data with service providers and partners*—To develop a CEA solution, a fair amount of customer data may need to be shared with third parties. This may include an offshore software testing organization, subcontractors providing design or development services, or third parties testing joint solutions using monetized customer data. In some cases, a mechanism used for data sharing, such as cookies on the web browser, may be openly available to others.

On the flip side, while privacy management is a big issue, there are several reasons why privacy may be a solvable problem:

- Only 5 to 7 percent of customer data is sensitive. While customer name and address may be sensitive information, ZIP+4 information is very public. Although it may be an invasion of privacy to divulge my location, it is fair to use location data from hundreds of drivers to predict congestion on a highway.
- Micro-segments can be generated by removing personal information from individual records and looking for patterns. If we strip patient name from a record, we can use the characteristics to study the outbreak of a disease.
- Customers can opt-in to share personal information in specific situations for specific purposes. I may provide information about my location to find the closest Starbucks.

In this chapter, I discuss how privacy policies can be specifically defined to protect customer privacy based on regulatory and corporate guidelines and how CEA information architecture can then be implemented, protecting and governing customer data using the policies. The resulting system is respectful of the privacy concerns while at the same time providing information about customers to the users of data.

Privacy Management: Functional Overview and Examples

The most visible public example of privacy management is the Amazon.com recommendation engine. Every time I go to search for a book, it provides me with helpful information regarding the purchase behavior of others who bought the book I am looking at. This information is generated from past orders. By analyzing who is buying which book, but removing sensitive information regarding customer name, address, and credit card information, Amazon has given me a useful piece of information without divulging any private information.

Now, let us take privacy to the next level of user permission. By writing a review for a book, I implicitly give Amazon permission to let others know my views of the book. For each review, Amazon is notified whether the reviewer has used his or her real name and whether it is a verified purchase review.

When a product review is marked "Amazon Verified Purchase," it means that the customer who wrote the review purchased the item at Amazon.com. Customers can add this label to their review only if they can verify that they bought the item they are reviewing from Amazon.com. Customers reading an Amazon Verified Purchase review can use this information to help them decide which reviews are most helpful in their purchasing decisions. If a review is not marked Amazon Verified Purchase, it does not mean that the reviewer has no experience with the product; it just means it could not be verified whether it had been purchased at Amazon. The reviewer might have purchased the item elsewhere or had some other interaction with it. If we could somehow validate the reviewer's experience with the product, we certainly would. The Amazon Verified Purchase label offers one more way to help gauge the quality and relevance of a product review.[45]

Recommendation engines can use a variety of buying information to provide additional help to shoppers. In addition to product-based clustering (as described above), a recommendation engine may also provide demographic or other segmentation information about other buyers if available—their ages, hobbies, ZIP+4 level location, and so on. However, if a recommendation engine were to provide me with specific names of people, it must first seek their permission to be a reference.

Privacy management works in a variety of ways to manage the flow of information to authorized individuals. The primary capabilities are described below:

- *Privacy Policy*—A documented policy regarding data privacy, identifying data that must be kept private and who is authorized to access that data. Depending on the level of sophistication, the policy may be a written document to be interpreted by the IT organization or an automated system using a privacy tool that administers privacy based on the policy.
- *Data Discovery*—The process of checking for privacy information. This process could be non-trivial in badly documented or older systems where the data model has been modified repeatedly. Data discovery may also find privacy information embedded in unstructured data, such as emails.
- *Privacy control system*—A process or automated system for managing data privacy by devising the mechanism for selective data access by user type or specific user names. The privacy control system uses the data privacy classification, each of which specifies who is authorized to access the data.
- *Data masking*—A system process of removing private information from the databases ("data at rest") or data streams ("data in motion"). Data masking uses a set of algorithms to remove specific data items without changing the integrity of information for the information system for which it is intended. For example, if we were to substitute "XXX" in place of customer name, it might be perfectly fine for a recommendation engine displaying ordering history for other buyers; but it might not be adequate for a data quality application looking for duplicate names. A number of domain- and context-specific data masking algorithms have emerged that retain most of the data without any private information.
- *Audit and Reporting*—A mechanism for reporting to management how privacy has been managed and its related audit function to review and test whether privacy management is adequate for the business purpose.

Privacy Management: Selective Deep Dive

A fair amount of data can be shared openly as long as it does not contain customer sensitive information. The task of data masking is to remove customer sensitive information without losing the data content needed for the application. In this section, we explore the data challenges around data masking and how technology has evolved to provide capabilities that can effectively protect customers while giving marketers sufficient information for a variety of marketing purposes. There are obvious limits to data masking, but a fair amount of ground can be covered via data masking.

Data masking essentially involves replacing original data with new data that destroys the content. For example, if I take a phone number and randomize the digits, the resulting phone number can be stored with my record and now the record can be freely shipped to any business partner or supplier without risk of divulging my phone number. We can apply the same treatment to the customer name, credit-card number, Social Security number, street address, or any other customer sensitive information (see Figure 10.1 for an example). If a customer purchased a set of goods, we are free to openly divulge the set of goods, so long as we do not mention the customer name without customer permission, as it happens on Amazon.com. What is the downside of data masking? The process may fail in a number of ways and requires careful design for successful data masking.

Figure 10.1: Data Masking Example

The data item may carry information that is critical for downstream processes. For example, in the United States the phone number carries area code and central office exchange information in the first six digits. If a marketing analytics system is tallying number of customers in different geographical regions using area code information for their landline phones, the area code must be preserved by data masking. Obviously, this is no longer a criterion for cell phones or Voice Over Internet Protocol (VOIP) phones, but it is an important consideration for a local landline phone.

If the address is masked, a downstream system using the address to compute local tax information would no longer be accurate. This information can be maintained by retaining ZIP+4 and masking the rest (street number and so on). A masking of customer names may lead to incorrect identification for a marketer that uses customer names to identify ethnic background. In most cases, customer names that maintain ethnic identities can be used to mask. These dependencies must be caught in the data flows, and appropriate data masking algorithms can be selected so that critical data needed for downstream systems is preserved.

Often, the customer name, phone number, or Social Security number may be used as a key. Data masking may in this case create unconnected records lacking referential integrity. A good example of this is the phone number. While masking a set of CRM and billing systems, I found 60 tables that used phone number as a key. We had to create a data masking algorithm that retained the referential integrity of these 60 tables while masking the phone numbers. We have recently been awarded a patent for the data masking algorithm used for this purpose.

Data masking must retain statistical inferences. The frequencies and correlations in the original data must match those of the masked data. This is not a problem until we start masking one of the core data items to be used in the statistical analysis. Data masking must retain the statistical inferences in the original data.

While data architects might have a field day discussing data flows, dependencies, and the impact of data masking, the important question is whether the resulting data will lead to any customer surprises. If, despite careful masking, we create an application that a customer perceives as giving away his or her identity, we have failed the test. In our work, we often combine legal and technical talent to come together for privacy policy decisions, so that the resulting policy is sound both from a business and technical perspective.

PART THREE:

How to Package a Customer Experience Analytics Program

11

Business Case for Customer Experience Analytics

CEA is a journey. What may be a bleeding-edge capability for one company or industry may be the base-level criteria for staying in business for another. In this chapter, I dive into a maturity model that allows us to measure the milestones in this journey, so we can benchmark a company in comparison to its peers. I will enumerate some of the business capabilities provided by CEA and discuss how the maturity model can be applied to each capability area.

While the initial business cases were primarily associated with productivity gains and cost reduction, we are increasingly seeing this area mature toward revenue enhancement and competitive value. While it is critical to have a tangible and credible roadmap and business value statement for CEA, this task has been "hit or miss" for many organizations. The Information Agenda team has invested considerably in asset development in this area. I will establish the framework for business case development to support a systematic approach to CEA program definition.

Drivers

Drivers are either internal or external forces that drive senior management priorities. For a commercial enterprise, factors such as revenue, cost, and customer acquisition and retention are typical drivers for its management to drive the organization's market valuation. For a government entity, the welfare and protection of citizens are typical drivers for analytics. For financial institutions, risk management is a key driver. Three major drivers are responsible for the popularity of CEA:

- Enable new services and business models
- Manage and differentiate the customer experience
- Improve efficiencies and reduce cost

Enable New Services and Business Models

In IBM's annual CEO surveys, we find creative business leaders are 15 percent more likely to innovate using enterprise models to deliver greater value by rethinking what is done in-house and by collaborating. They are 10 percent more likely to rethink the industry model by moving into a new industry or creating an entirely new industry. These creative leaders are also 20 percent more likely to generate revenue models via new value propositions and new pricing models.[46]

CEA provides an avenue for innovation, supplying insights toward new services and business models. Many organizations are experimenting with intelligent campaigns that improve product sales or usage by focusing on micro-segments and offering campaigns at the point of sale to a specific individual belonging to a micro-segment. Analytics provides the insights to segment the customers, to identify a customer belonging to a micro-segment, and to design the campaign best-suited to this individual. Usage analytics results in new insights on how customers buy. The Amazon recommendation engine is an example of how usage information is used for up-selling to similar customers. Also, use of analytics has prompted a food chain where customer and usage data can be collated, anonymized, and monetized for reuse by others.

Manage and Differentiate the Customer Experience

All customers are not equal. Most corporations use analytics to identify the highest volume or most profitable customers and use a combination of differentiated services, policies, and discounts to provide higher-quality products or services to their most important customers. Airlines were one of the early adopters of loyalty points for frequent flyers. The customer experience in the airline industry is now far more differentiated for airlines' best customers across all touch points.

Many other industries are beginning to differentiate products and services. However, finding these customers may not be that simple across divisional silos and duplicated customer records. Master Data Management provides tools for identifying the best customers. Social networks and call patterns across customers can also be used to identify social opinion leaders. These are individuals who most often communicate with a large group of people and are also in the best position to influence their purchase behavior. Analytics has shown that as social leaders churn, they most often carry their group of customers to the competition with them.

Improve Efficiencies and Reduce Cost

Analytics can be used to improve efficiencies of the customer-facing processes while maintaining customer experience. The customer-facing processes can be optimized to provide the best service to customers based on their importance. Analytics can be used to improve revenue assurance and fraud detection.

In a roadmap, it is often advantageous to build a program that supports a portfolio of drivers, with varying levels of quantification. We can use cost reduction as a way to fund the CEA program and then use qualitative information on new services, new revenues, and improved customer experience to sell to the senior management. While these are important issues for competitiveness of an organization in the marketplace, they are also the most difficult to quantify and justify. In many cases, we developed roadmaps and justified the programs using cost reduction, while mentioning the larger benefits. Once we had implemented the programs, the revenue increases were nice surprises and were used by management to continue with the programs despite budget cuts and program reductions elsewhere.

Capabilities

Capabilities represent a collection of business processes, people, and technology for a specific purpose.[47] For example, a financial institution may place a risk management function for loan approval. The risk management would require technology components for statistical analysis and modeling, a set of trained people who can assemble risk management information from a variety of sources, and a risk management process that starts with risk data and ends with a score for a customer.

Analytics supports a number of key capabilities in response to drivers. In the past five years, these capabilities have become increasingly sophisticated, as well as automated. Also, many CEA-driven capabilities are inter-organizational, as they use business partnership between companies in different industries. For example, use of loyalty points to reward credit-card purchases requires collaboration between a bank and an airline. As the amount of data has grown, so have the tools for faster data collection and real-time analytics. These tools have enabled a whole set of new capabilities. Let us examine a set of analytics-supported capabilities to support typical drivers (also see Figure 11.1).

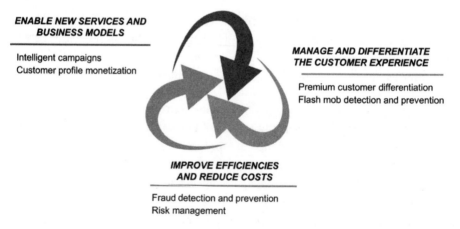

ENABLE NEW SERVICES AND BUSINESS MODELS

Intelligent campaigns
Customer profile monetization

MANAGE AND DIFFERENTIATE THE CUSTOMER EXPERIENCE

Premium customer differentiation
Flash mob detection and prevention

IMPROVE EFFICIENCIES AND REDUCE COSTS

Fraud detection and prevention
Risk management

Figure 11.1: Business drivers and capabilities for customer experience analytics

Marketing campaigns in the past were typically organized for large customer segments, deployed via network TV advertising or newspaper advertisements, and meant for an entire geographical or demographic segment. In contrast, "intelligent campaigns" are personalized to micro-segments or individuals and communicated via personal communication—email, SMS message, and so on—to a specific customer. I may use an intelligent campaign to target prepaid wireless customers who are about to run out of minutes on their prepaid cards and direct them to a nearby store that is carrying the prepaid cards. The intelligent campaign employs customer billing details, usage information, and customer location to deliver a specific communication to a specific customer under a specific set of conditions. Unlike the campaigns of the past, thousands of micro-campaigns can be executed each day, each personalized to a set of customers and fine-tuned based on success rate. Micro-campaigns can drive new services and new business models and typically will impact revenues.

In Chapter 1, I discussed a retail scenario associated with intelligent location-based coupon distribution. A communications service provider (CSP) may partner with a retailer to offer specific grocery coupons to a customer targeted via "Customer Profile Monetization." The customer profile and location information may be harvested out of the CSP's databases and offered to the retailer. The retailer offers specific coupons to a customer. The coupon may be delivered via smart phone carried by the customer at the time the customer enters the grocery store. In this case, Customer Profile Monetization is a capability offered by the CSP. It includes technology for harvesting customer profile information from a variety of sources, including customer residential location, travel patterns, television watching patterns, Internet usage, billing details, and other data. Some of this information may be considered private and the monetization may include a privacy filter that disallows sharing information unless authorized by the customer. This is another example of a new service and business model, as it involves a partnership between a CSP and a retailer.

In the Introduction, I discussed how airlines and others are providing differentiated services to premium customers. A premium customer is one who is using the services more frequently than the average customer, and hence provides a lot more revenue to the service provider. This could include someone buying many products or using a metered product more heavily. Once a premium customer has been identified, the service provider may incorporate the identification tags in all customer-facing processes, so that any one dealing with this customer, whether a person or an autonomous agent, is aware of premium customers and provides a set of services not usually provided to other customers. The capability involves technology and processes for identifying premium customers, including harmonization or matching of customer data across different customer databases and a mechanism for placing this information in every touch point so it can alter policies and procedures. It also includes a process for premium customers and awareness among employees regarding the policies for premium customers.

We described "flash mobs" in Chapter 1, which lead to group behavior for both good and bad intentions. If flash mobs are being used for criminal purposes, law enforcement agencies require capabilities to detect and prevent rioting flash mobs from raiding neighborhood stores. Such capabilities include detection of flash mob activity in social media and communications devices, use of privacy management to ensure the detection and prevention process is done in a legally proper way, and alerting local police regarding a potential flash mob formation.

Measurements

Measurements are used to quantify the progress of a capability and its impact. With the increasing automation in products and processes, we now have many more ways to measure the effective functioning of a capability. These measurements can be visualized using a business value tree, such as the sample business value tree shown in Figure 11.2.

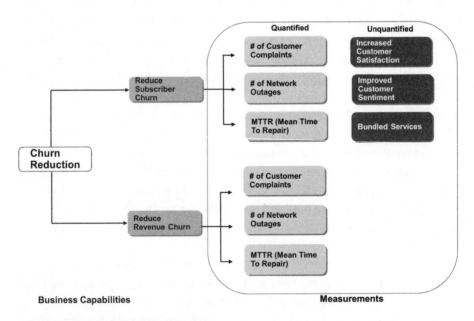

Figure 11.2: Sample business value tree

As we evaluate an analytics program, we can visualize the capabilities required and their impact, thereby allowing management to prioritize program spending based on capabilities that have the biggest impact to the organization. Measurements are used to link business capabilities to drivers. Value trees can also be used to identify common capabilities that impact multiple measurements. Value trees can be used to track benefits by program phases, identifying capabilities enabled by a particular phase. We can also maintain the best practices toward each capability to estimate the impact of a capability using past case studies.

Business Maturity Levels

As I stated earlier, CEA is a journey and can be implemented using a number of iterative phases, each advancing the capability via well-defined yet small steps to reduce risk. The Information Agenda team has observed a large number of analytics programs worldwide and has developed a set of benchmarks for analytics at different levels of maturity. This has been captured using a business maturity model that allows us to specify current and target levels of maturity and what can be achieved in each phase. The model has four levels of maturity.

- *Breakaway*—A company that is generally considered to be the best in the class in its execution of key business strategies, able to exhibit the characteristics of an agile, transformational, and optimized organization. This classification excludes "bleeding-edge" or pioneering aspects; however, these may also be evident in such companies. Key predictive performance indicators are used in modeling for outcomes, and information is utilized enterprise-wide for multidimensional decision-making.
- *Differentiating*—A company whose execution of key business strategies through utilization of information is viewed as generally better than most other companies, creating a degree of sustainable competitive advantage. Management has the ability to adapt to changes to the business to a degree, as well as measure business performance. Business leaders and users have visibility to key information and metrics for effective decision-making.

- *Competitive*—A company whose capabilities generally are in line with the majority of similar companies, with a growing ability to make decisions on how to create competitive advantage. This maturity level is also the starting point to establish some consistency in key business metrics across the enterprise.
- *Foundational*—A company whose capabilities to gather key information generally lag behind the majority of peers, which could potentially result in a competitive disadvantage. Information is not consistently available or utilized to make enterprise-wide business decisions. A degree of manual efforts to gather information is still required.
- *Ad hoc*—A company that is just starting to develop capability to gather consistent information in key functional areas, generally falling well behind other companies in the corresponding sector. Information beyond basic reporting is not available. Time-consuming, manual efforts are generally required to gather the information needed for day-to-day business decisions.

This model is an important tool in developing an enterprise-wide analytics roadmap. It allows us to specify specific capabilities developed in each phase, compare them with others in the industry and align metrics to each level, so that the benefits can be identified using the metrics and can be quantified using either benchmarks or company-specific information.

The business maturity model lets us rapidly quantify the benefits of a CEA program. We have been tracking actual benefits using case studies and using these benchmarks in roadmap development. The maturity models and their underlying descriptions are industry-specific, as implementations and benefits differ from one industry to the next.

We have developed business maturity models for a number of CEA use cases. Table 11.1 shows one such example, for "Bill Shock Analytics."

	Ad hoc	Foundational	Competitive	Differentiating	Breakaway
Capability: Provide alert to customers	Customer sees the charges first time in the bill	A monthly utilization summary	Web- and device-based interface to display usage with one day delay	Alert after each session with extraordinary usage	Predict usage and seek permission during usage
Measurements					
Impact on call centers	Baseline	0% to 1% reduction	10% reduction	10% reduction	10% reduction
Reduction in collection costs	Baseline	0% to 1% reduction	5% reduction	20% reduction	30% reduction
Reduction in bad debt	Baseline	0% to 1% reduction	5% reduction	20% reduction	30% reduction
Improvement in customer satisfaction	Baseline	0% to 1% reduction	5% improvement	7-8% improvement	10-12% improvement
Churn reduction	Baseline	0% to 1% reduction	5% improvement	7-8% improvement	10-12% improvement

Table 11.1: Business maturity model for bill shock analytics

Most of us have been through a bill shock. For many international travelers, bill shock is associated with international roaming charges or international data charges. For residential subscribers, it could result from movie or music downloads in limited data plans. A telecommunications service provider typically offers services using a pricing model. As a post-paid subscriber uses these services, the charges are incremented and are available to the subscriber. In many cases, subscribers do not monitor their charges as they use the services, but only review the charges once they receive the bill. If the bill turns out to be much higher than expected, it leads to "bill shock" in the customer experience and could result in customer churn or bad debt.

Analytics can be used at various levels of maturity to make the bill more transparent to the subscriber and to make the monitoring closer to usage. Implementation of Bill Shock Analytics is not trivial, as it involves billing systems and rating engines with various levels of delays in collecting and analyzing data. It also requires tools for summarizing alert information and providing it to the subscriber within a reasonable time to affect usage. Each level of maturity results in different levels of impacts on collection costs, bad debt, customer satisfaction, and churn.

Summary

In this chapter, we covered business parameters, value trees, and Business Maturity Models. These are tools for constructing a roadmap for CEA. We anticipate developing these maturity models around maturing use cases and associated key performance indicators (KPIs) around the globe, covering different markets and different environments, which will help us provide business value statements using industry examples. However, we are also finding rapid changes in the implementation of CEA across the globe, with new use cases and new business models which have not been tried before. As a result, this field will evolve as we fully digest massive parallel platforms providing real-time analytics using social media and other external data.

12

CHAPTER

Conclusions

Automation in product engineering and touch points and associated formation of the CEA marketplace are creating a tsunami of data in a number of related industries. This is leading to one of the most disruptive forces in the marketplace/social order. Consumers are rapidly becoming more sophisticated, leading to major social changes and rapid swings in market shares. Let me summarize the role CEA plays in these changes.

This book has provided an overview of CEA. I began in Part 1 with a series of scenarios to identify the basic features of CEA that were common across industries—telecommunications, media and entertainment, financial services, health, industrial, public services, travel, and others. These features and trends were then used to establish the business opportunity for CEA. In Part 2, I outlined the architecture components of a CEA solution, consisting of Master Data Management, stream computing, predictive modeling, analytics engine, and privacy management. In Part 3, I outlined how an organization can build a roadmap for CEA.

Market Forces

Let us summarize the three market forces. First of all, automation is sweeping several industries, as we discussed in Chapters 1 and 2. These changes stem from product engineering, touch point automation, and changes to the supply chain. Products are increasingly electronic, giving us an opportunity to instrument customer experience. This massive volume and variety of instrumented experience information can be used to improve product and customer experience. The closed-loop interaction between customer experience and product automation is reducing product life cycles, creating new opportunities, and rapidly changing competitive positions of suppliers in the marketplace. It is also creating new opportunities for innovation in health care, forcing new requirements for city governments in crime prevention, and paving new ways to prevent fraud in many industries.

Next, the availability of customer data is creating new markets for buying and selling customer information across industries. Customer data can be collated, packaged, and resold to other industries. Alternatively, organizations in different industries can band together to improve overall customer experience, as in the travel industry. As we witness these disruptive changes, the bystanders in this change will be forced to play a commodity role. Cable and telecommunication companies are seeing a tsunami of data on their pipes with no significant increase in revenue, while new products are flowing to device makers—navigation devices, video players, smart phones, and others.

The real impact on the consumer is increasingly felt by the suppliers in the form of customer sophistication. The power of referral and social media is dwarfing other forms of persuasions. Rating on Yelp is carrying an increasingly larger role compared with traditional advertising. It is also creating new ways of social interaction—both positive and negative. While social media is allowing us to be more knowledgeable about others' customer experience, it is also increasingly organizing crime and social unrest.

The CEA Solution

I detailed the technical solution to establish a CEA solution. The solution has two components: an above-the-line real-time component and a below-the-line historical analysis component. The real-time, streaming component operates at real-time or near real-time speed to analyze, score, and act upon streaming customer experience data. The historical analysis component logs samples of streaming information and uses predictive modeling to analyze the history to predict future behavior. The historical analysis provides the mechanism to change the real-time component, thereby providing an adaptive analytics engine that can react to streaming data at blazing speeds while at the same time changing its behavior with short-, medium-, and long-term trends. This architecture is supported by five major architecture components.

First, the data integration and Master Data Management component provides the massively parallel platform to ingest data, harmonize across multiple sources to correlate data for a single customer, and make it ready for analytics. The massively parallel platform can work on many processors simultaneously to support massive volumes of input data. As the sizes of input data have grown, the parallel processing capabilities have kept up with our ability to process this data at low-level latency. The matching algorithms have provided ways to correlate both inter- and intra-organizational data using sophisticated fuzzy logic, thereby creating a single view of the customer to analyze, predict, and act upon customer experience.

Second, stream computing provides analysis capabilities in real-time and near real-time. These tools provide ways to look for patterns in streaming data, forming complex windows, stitching experience information across disparate sources, and working in a massively parallel mode like its data integration counter parts. Stream computing has taken complex event processing to the next level of evolution, where analytics has successfully kept up with the increase in the volume and variety of structured and unstructured data.

Third, analytics engines have supplied the capabilities to store historical information and provide an integrated platform for reporting, analytics, and predictive modeling. The data can be rapidly stored, retrieved, and used for ad hoc queries and advanced analytics. Analytics engines are specially engineered to work in massively parallel mode to deal with large volumes of data and use far simpler data models to allow query and modeling without the overhead of a traditional data warehouse platform.

Fourth, the predictive modeling component packs sophisticated modeling and statistical analysis with sophisticated collaboration and deployment tools to promote and use the models. The models are designed on the predictive modeling platform, using enormous data crunching abilities on the specially designed analytics engine and documented using PMML to share with the real-time environment. The collaboration and deployment tools track the success of the models in the real-world and provide a mechanism for experiment design and model retirement based on changing conditions.

Last but not the least, privacy management gives customers the assurance that their private data will be closely managed and not inadvertently released to unauthorized parties. The privacy management component enables us to establish privacy policies and monitor their use in protecting customer data. Data masking lets us shield sensitive data from being shared as information is packaged, analyzed, and consumed.

The Power of CEA

Let us now use these three market forces and five architectural components as a lens to re-examine some of the scenarios described in Chapter 1. The first scenario described telecommunications service levels and how a communications service provider can collect and analyze customer experience data to identify poor service quality and use communication with the customer to resolve the problems. I used two scenarios, one involving the Steve Jobs iPhone demonstration and the other relating to my broadband service at home. The power of CEA in these cases is derived from the automation in product engineering. The end-user devices, as well as the communications network, generate a wide variety of event information that can be used to identify service problems. The breakthrough in these scenarios came from the capability to relate a network problem to a specific customer or set of customers and the ability to prioritize customer communication based on customer importance. In the case of both Steve Jobs and my residential service, the problems were easily identifiable. What was difficult and expensive was the attention to be given to the specific customer. The call I received was a great example of matching service quality to a specific customer and initiating calls to specific customers who were most important and had the highest propensity to churn.

The financial services scenario started with mortgage lending and related risk analysis and ended with connecting credit-card and cell phone location. Between the three scenarios, it covered two market forces. The automation in customer self-service resulted in customer data associated with different mortgage accounts, which was used by the service provider to match the customer information. The risk analysis can use a lot of third-party–provided information available publicly. If a credit-card issuer would use cell phone information to verify customer presence at a credit-card transaction site, this would be an excellent example of customer information from one industry being sold and reused in another industry. The solution would require Master Data Management for matching multiple customer accounts, Hadoop for assembling risk information from public data available regarding individuals, stream computing for identifying patterns of customer presence, and predictive modeling for risk management and credit-card fraud detection using an analytics engine.

The public services flash mob scenario shows the dark side of customer sophistication. Criminals are increasingly using telecommunications and social media to organize crime. Law enforcement organizations require stream computing to identify a buzz of criminal activity. Very often, it is hard to identify this buzz; sophisticated predictive modeling and scoring engines are required to detect and differentiate between diversion tactics used by criminals as decoys versus real plans to congregate in a spot for criminal purposes. This is also a topic of great debate on privacy management. What is the privacy policy? Which sources can law enforcement monitor without court approval? We should expect this area to evolve in legal and regulatory terms as the democracies and autocracies around the world grapple with positive and negative examples of informal social organization.

The healthcare examples depict automation and our capabilities to push the envelope in using Master Data Management and stream computing in life-preserving, real-time situations.

CEA enables an organization to act as personably and empathetically to the customer as organizations did in customer interactions 50 years ago, while at the same time using technology to offer these capabilities globally 24x7 and consistently to a sophisticated, networked customer base. Customer data must be organized, and it must be correlated across organizational silos and also across industries to make insightful discoveries about customer profiles. Airlines were the first ones to team up with credit-card companies to share loyalty points. Phone companies can share location information with credit-card companies to differentiate between legitimate and fraudulent uses of credit cards.

These capabilities face a number of challenges in the area of privacy management and regulations. Predators are ready to misuse the information. At the same time, the use of private data in a controlled opt-in setting is a very valued addition to the customer. A number of market leaders have successfully used a combination of opt-in and data masking to offer CEA-driven game-changer capabilities. This area is also subject to a fair amount of regulatory scrutiny and changes.

CEA is an enabler to a series of capabilities that offer disruptive changes. In many cases, these capabilities are redrawing competitive maps, wiping out established organizations, and replacing them with new ones. It will be interesting to see how leaders will use CEA as a strategic weapon to stay ahead of these changes.

List of Abbreviations

ACID	Atomicity, Consistency, Isolation, and Durability
ARRA	American Recovery and Reinvestment Act
BPM	Business Process Management
CDI	Customer Data Integration
CDR	Call Detail Record
CEA	Customer Experience Analytics
CMO	Chief Marketing Officer
CRM	Customer Relationship Management
CSP	Communications Service Provider
DMG	Data Mining Group
EMPI	Enterprise Master Patient Index
ERP	Enterprise Resource Planning
ETL	Extract, Transform, and Load
FPGA	Field-Programmable Gate Array
GPS	Global Positioning System
HA/DR	High Availability/Disaster Recovery
HIE	Health Information Exchange
ICU	Intensive Care Unit
IPO	Initial Public Offering
IT	Information Technology
IVR	Interactive Voice Response
KPI	Key Performance Indicator
MPP	Massively Parallel Processing
NBA	Next Best Action

NCAG	National Consumer Assets Group
NICU	Neonatal Intensive Care Unit
PA-SIIS	Pennsylvania Statewide Immunization Information System
PE	Processing Element
PIM	Product Information Management
PMML	Predictive Model Markup Language
R&D	Research and Development
SLA	Service Level Agreement
SMP	Symmetric Multiprocessing
SMS	Short Message Service
SPL	Streams Processing Language
SPU	Snippet Processing Unit
STP	Straight Through Processing
UOIT	University of Ontario Institute of Technology
UPMC	University of Pittsburgh Medical Center
VOIP	Voice Over Internet Protocol
WWDC	Worldwide Developing Conference

Notes

1. "Today's CMO: Innovating or Following?" IBM Institute of Business Value, IBM 2011.
2. Fred Wiersema. *How to Design a Great Customer Experience*. FT Press, 2010.
3. Thomas H. Davenport and Jeanne G. Harris, *Competing on Analytics*. Harvard Business School Press, 2007.
4. https://www.chase.com/online/services/check-deposit.htm.
5. "Flash mobs pose challenge to police tactics." *USA Today*, http://www.usatoday.com/news/nation/2011-08-18-flash-mobs-police_n.htm?csp=34news.
6. http://www-03.ibm.com/press/us/en/pressrelease/24694.wss.
7. http://www-03.ibm.com/press/us/en/pressrelease/34574.wss.
8. Dr. Carolyn McGregor. *Neonatal Health Informatics: Uncharted Discovery*. University of Waterloo Seminar Series, May 27, 2009.
9. "Want low premiums? Let insurers 'drive' with you" (Editorial). *USA Today*. http://www.usatoday.com/news/opinion/editorials/2011-08-18-car-insurance-drivers-tracking_n.htm.
10. "Another view: Steer clear of the cars that spy" (Editorial). *USA Today*. http://www.usatoday.com/news/opinion/editorials/2011-08-18-car-insurance-monitors-driving-snapshot_n.htm.
11. R. Johri and Z. Filipi. *Self-Learning Neural Controller for Hybrid Power Management Using Neuro-Dynamic Programming*. SAE Technical Paper, 011-24-0081, 2011.

12. R. Johri, A. Salvi, and Z. Filipi. *Optimal Energy Management for a Hybrid Vehicle Using Neuro-Dynamic Programming to Consider Transient Engine Operation.* Dynamic Systems and Control Conference, Arlington, Virginia, 2011.

13. "TomTom launches the world's most accurate live traffic map." http://corporate.tomtom.com/releasedetail.cfm?ReleaseID=558648.

14. Robert J. Meyer and Arvind Sathi. "A Multi-Attribute Model of Consumer Choice During Product Learning," *Marketing Science*, Volume 4, Number 1 (Winter 1985).

15. Martha Rogers and Don Peppers. *The One to One Future* (Kindle Locations 141–142). Crown Business. Kindle Edition, 2000-01-07.

16. "Price Optimization Models." Bain and Company. http://www.bain.com/publications/articles/management-tools-2011-price-optimization-models.aspx.

17. Batty et al. "Predictive Modeling for Life Insurance," Deloitte Consulting, 2010. http://www.soa.org/files/pdf/research-pred-mod-life-batty.pdf.

18. David Court, Dave Elzinga, Susan Mulder, and Ole Jørgen Vetvik, "The Consumer Decision Journey," *McKinsey Quarterly*, June 2009. https://www.mckinseyquarterly.com/The_consumer_decision_journey_2373.

19. http://www.checkfacebook.com.

20. http://blog.nielsen.com/nielsenwire/wp-content/uploads/2009/07/pr_global-study_07709.pdf.

21. "A foreign mobile communications provider." IBM Research Case Study. http://domino.watson.ibm.com/odis/odis.nsf/pages/case.43.html.

22. http://www.iab.net/about_the_iab/recent_press_releases/press_release_archive/press_release/pr-041311.

23. http://www.yelp.com.

24. Amir Efrati, "Online Ads: Where 1,240 Companies Fit In," *Wall Street Journal*, June 6, 2011.

25. http://freshnetworks.com/blog/2011/03/twitter-numbers-and-statistics.

26. Amir Efrati and Jennifer Valentino-DeVries. "Computers, Too, Can Give Away Location." *Wall Street Journal*, April 27, 2011.

27. Jennifer Velentino-DeVries, "Law Makers Seek Limits on Location Data Use." *Wall Street Journal*, June 15, 2011.

28. Allen Dreibelbis, Eberhard Hechler, Ivan Milman, Martin Oberhofer, Paul van Run, and Dan Wolfson. *Enterprise Master Data Management, An SOA Approach to Managing Core Information.* IBM Press, 2008.

29. John Radcliffe. "Gartner's Seven Building Blocks of MDM: The Foundation of Successful MDM." http://www.gartner.com/it/content/1333900/1333913/may_26_master_data_mgmt_jradcliffe.pdf.
30. Ibid. Slide 18.
31. Initiate Inspector is a trademark of IBM.
32. Schulte. *Event Processing: Designing IT Systems for Agile Companies* (Kindle Locations 1116–1121). McGraw-Hill Osborne Media. Kindle Edition, 2009.
33. http://www-01.ibm.com/software/data/bigdata.
34. Tom White. *Hadoop: The Definitive Guide* (pp. 1–2). O'Reilly Media. Kindle Edition, 2009-05-29.
35. Robert Lee Hotz, "The Really Smart Phone." *Wall Street Journal*, April 23, 2011.
36. http://www.redbooks.ibm.com/redpapers/pdfs/redp4710.pdf.
37. Gordon S. Linoff. *Data Mining Techniques: For Marketing, Sales, and Customer Relationship Management* (Kindle Location 757). Wiley Computer Publishing. Kindle Edition, 2011.
38. *IBM SPSS Predictive Analytics: Optimizing Decisions at the Point of Impact*, Redbook, IBM, 2010.
39. http://www.dmg.org.
40. http://www.dataupia.com/pdfs/industryanalysts/reg/Data_Management_Appliances.pdf.
41. http://www.netezza.com/releases/2009/release121709.htm.
42. http://www.catalinamarketing.com/pdf/informationweek-full-issue-august-9-2010_3791.pdf.
43. http://blog.connectedplanetonline.com/unfiltered/2011/06/29/t-mobile-crunching-17-billion-transactions-a-day-%E2%80%93-what-does-it-do-with-all-that-data.
44. http://www.netezza.com/documents/whitepapers/Sandia_Labs_White_Paper_July_06.pdf.
45. http://www.amazon.com/gp/community-help/amazon-verified-purchase.
46. "Capitalizing on Business Complexity: Insights from the Global Chief Executive Officer Study." IBM Institute of Business Value, IBM web site, 2010.
47. Ric Merrifield, Jack Calhoun, and Dennis Stevens. "The Next Revolution in Productivity." *Harvard Business Review*, June 2008.